PRAISE FOR TICK TICK DOLLAR™

'Your personal story is very impressive. You have clearly lived the purpose, passion, performance logic you write about.'
Dave Ulrich - World's #1 Management Guru
Author of 'Leadership Brand'

'In my bestselling book Triggers', I raised this important question. Why don't we become the person we really want to be? In his book, 'Tick Tick Dollar', Qaier gives us the answer to this question and shares his proven philosophy to make that life a reality'
Marshall Goldsmith - World's #1 Leadership Coach
#1 New York Times Bestselling Author of TRIGGERS'

'Qaiser Abbas is a Remarkable Teacher'
Tony Buzan – World's #1 Creativity Guru
Inventor of MindMaps

'Oaiser is the future of motivational speaking. He is an inspiration to millions around the globe.'
Brian Tracy – World' #1 Personal Development Guru
Author of bestseller 'Eat That Frog'

BESTSELLING BOOKS BY QAISER ABBAS

- **Speed Coaching**™
  Leaders' Playbook for Powerful Coaching Conversations

- **Power of Teams**
  Building High-Performance, Result-Oriented Teams

- **Made in Crises**
  Tested Strategies for Leading in Turbulent Times

- **Leadership Insights**
  Success Strategies from Top Business Leaders – (co-authored with Amer Qureshi)

- **The Vocabulary of Greatness**™
  Your 6-Word Guide for Lasting Success

- **Tick Tick Dollar**
  14 Principles of Peak Performance

TICK TICK DOLLAR™

14 PRINCIPLES OF PEAK PERFORMANCE

QAISER ABBAS

BALBOA.PRESS

A DIVISION OF HAY HOUSE

Balboa Press books may be ordered through booksellers or by contacting:

Balboa Press
A Division of Hay House
1663 Liberty Drive
Bloomington, IN 47403
www.balboapress.com
844-682-1282

Print information available on the last page.

ISBN: 978-1-9822-5190-1 (sc)
ISBN: 978-1-9822-5189-5 (e)

Balboa Press rev. date: 08/07/2020

All author's proceeds will go to Possibilities
Foundation to educate underprivileged children

To
Hussain
Zainab
&
Ghazi

ABOUT QAISER ABBAS

A Business Psychologist by education, Qaiser Abbas is an Award-Winning Leadership Coach, Motivational Speaker, and the author of 10 bestselling books, including 'Power of Teams.

World's #1 Leadership Coach, Dr. Marshall Goldsmith, has endorsed Qaiser's 'Dare Coaching Framework'™. He is the Master Mind behind one of the fastest-growing Coach-Networks, spread in four continents with over 250 Certified Coaches.

In his 20 years journey as Leadership Coach, Qaiser has had the privilege to coach CEOs, business leaders, celebrities and superstars of sports, movies, and media. His clients include Fortune 500 companies like Toyota, GE, Nestle, Philips, Total, Schlumberger, Coca Cola, PepsiCo, Unilever, Abbott, and Reckitt-Benckiser.

Qaiser is the recipient of the 'Brian Tracy International Excellence Award 2017, held in London. He is also the recipient of the 'Trainer of the Year' Award for Asia by the World HRD Congress, Singapore.

Apart from coaching and training leaders in the world's top MNCs, World Bank, WHO, and US Embassy, Qaiser is making a massive contribution to society through 'Possibilities Schools' and 'My First Bike.'

His 100% books proceeds support out-of-school children's education. To know more about him, you can visit <u>www.qaiserabbas.org</u> or <u>www.possibilities.net.pk</u>.

CONTENTS

FOREWORD BY
MARSHALL GOLDSMITH

Do you have the courage to take charge of your life, change the way you think and live a life you truly desire? If yes, Tick Tick Dollar guides you plainly in the right direction to lead the life you want to.

In my bestselling book '**Triggers,**' I raised this important question. 'Why don't we become the person we want to be?'. In his book, Tick Tick Dollar, Qaiser gives us his answer to this question and shares his proven philosophy to make that life a reality.

Qaiser and I share a similar passion and purpose, helping people become better. We both are on a journey to bring positive, measurable behavioral change in people's lives, making them, their teams, and stakeholders experience greater success, joy, and fulfillment.

Qaiser has been applying my Stakeholder Centered Coaching methodology successfully in his coaching and leadership practice, and he is a valuable member of my global network of coaches.

He brings enormous energy, passion, commitment, and, most importantly, his personal transformational story that has touched the heart of millions all over the world. His personal example distinguishes him from the scores of success coaches and speakers around him.

Over the past 20 years, Qaiser has successfully used his success principles with hundreds of people he has coached from all walks of life. Seeing his commitment to practice my coaching philosophy, he is a true ambassador of Marshall Goldsmith Stakeholder Cantered Coaching in Pakistan.

After having spent over 40 years in producing a positive, measurable change in human behavior, I am incredibly delighted to find a book that is so powerful in content yet so simple to practice. In this life-changing book, Qaiser presents two beautiful gifts to you. The first gift is his philosophy to live a more rewarding life. And the second is a set of principles you can use to turn your dreams into reality.

Qaiser is a living example of living his philosophy of purpose, passion, and performance. This philosophy has been his inspiration and guiding star to live a life that a mere couple of years ago, would have seemed outrageous even in his own farthest dreams.

Today, this unbelievably blessed life is a reality. From humble beginnings, making $18 a month to establishing his international management development and consulting company, *Possibilities*, and becoming a Globally Certified Coach in Marshall Goldsmith Stakeholder Centered Coaching; Tick Tick Dollar™ philosophy has been Qaiser's guide every single step of the way.

It doesn't matter whether you are already a superstar or feel lost; Tick Tick Dollar has the power to change your life. It is a *tried and true* recipe for creating the life you desire for yourself.

Tick Tick Dollar takes you beyond the traditional peak performance or success books. It is a mindset that challenges you to listen to your inner calling, redirect your enormous potential to move toward it, and live gracefully with an unquestionable legacy.

You will embark on a journey that gives free rein to your true potential. Your daily stresses, worries, and anxieties will be transformed into your allies to help you achieve breakthrough performances in significant areas of your life.

You will move away from excuses and start orchestrating positive changes in your life. You will get rid of the justifications, explanations, and rationalizations that have reinforced your unspoken belief that you are mediocre. You will stop *apologizing* and start living the life that is out there waiting for you.

Tick Tick Dollar™ will introduce a renewed sense of achievement and fulfillment in your life by focusing on what has real value for you. You will realize the importance and feel the urge to make better decisions while taking full charge of the results. Your mind will begin to experience freedom from irritating disturbances and achieve greater calm, serenity, and peace. The new choices will allow you to pick a healthier, happier, and more prosperous life.

Qaiser's core philosophy, in a nutshell, is this: Living every day with purpose and passion for high-performance guarantees achievement and fulfillment.

Only a 100% commitment to maximizing your purpose, passion, and performance will guarantee a measurable and sustainable change in your behavior. Starting today, living your purpose and passion for most exceptional performance must become the slogan of your life.

It is heartwarming to see how Qaiser is making a positive contributor to society through his exceptional project, Possibilities Schools, offering free education to thousands of underprivileged children of Pakistan. He is also the Founder of 'My First Bike,' a unique mission to gift underprivileged children their life's first bike through a unique and powerful learning experience.

The total income Qaiser generates from his books supports his back to social initiatives. Reading this book will change your life and the life of others at the same time.

It gives me great joy to see Qaiser's dedication, and I wish him all the best in his endeavor to make a positive change in society.

Marshall Goldsmith Ph.D.
World's #1 Leadership Coach

The American Management Association has recognized Dr. Marshall Goldsmith as one of the 50 greatest thinkers and business leaders who have impacted the field of management and leadership over the past 80 years. Business Week titled him as one of the most influential practitioners in leadership development history.

LIVE YOUR DREAMS
THE BACKSTORY STORY OF TICK TICK DOLLAR™

> *"The greater danger for most of us is not that our aim is too high and miss it, but that it is too low and we reach it."*
> Michelangelo

'If your dreams are high, and your beginnings are low, congratulations! Life is going to offer you something really, really BIG!' The speaker's passion had instantly injected a current of high-octane energy and anticipation in his audience. Some 1500 top executives from 100 countries at IFTDO's 43rd international conference at the expo center, Dubai, were utterly glued to the speaker.

'No worries if you aim for gold and miss it; the real worry would be when you aim for the bronze and get it.' The audience was completely enthralled by the powerful message of the charismatic speaker.

'Let me share a story with you. The story of a young child whose dreams were sky-high, but his beginnings were shallow.' The speaker's inspiring message held a firm promise to touch the hearts and souls of his audience.

He projected on to the screen the image of a little boy. His shining eyes were filled with a million dreams, carrying some magnetic power. His appearance, dress, and looks, however, contradicted the aspirations his eyes revealed.

'Yes, my friends! This child's dreams were as high as the K2, but his origins were more wretched than you could possibly imagine. He was born into a family that survived well below the poverty line. It was a family afflicted with hunger, deprivation, ill-health, inadequacy, and never-ending pain. He was the youngest among the eight children of hardworking, committed visionary parents. Despite having no formal education, his father was a symbol of dedication, self-reliance, and perseverance. But to the world, he was only a laborer.

'At the very young age of seven, he was deprived forever of his mother's tender love, care, and protection. The boy wept bitterly as he sat beside the lifeless body of his mother. Many years later, he was told that the mother's disease was curable. She died because the family had no money to afford treatment. But the dreams his dead mother had nurtured in him remained unshaken. Fire and passion were burning in him to raise the living standards of his family.'

The global leaders from the world's top companies present in the hall were captivated by the gripping story's spell.

'He was never able to wear the clothes his heart desired nor ever play with the toys he craved to have. Some wealthy relatives would hand over their used clothes to the poor family. The sensitive young boy would feel self-conscious and embarrassed. Facing the same relatives or the world at large wearing cast-off garments that were not even the right fit for him was a painful experience.

'Despite being promised rewards like a bike or some other coveted item for attaining the first position in his class, his family could never honor their commitments. The prime goal for the whole family was to scrape together enough to put a meal on the table every day. Paying the rent became almost an obsession for fear of losing the roof over their heads. The emotional turmoil prevailing in the family turned his elder brother into a drug addict. That was really the beginning of a series of unfortunate setbacks. But his dreams were still lofty. His determination to lift his family out of their miserable conditions grew stronger with every passing day.

As a young boy, he suffered from an acute lack of self-confidence, self-esteem, and trust. He was shy, timid, and withdrawn. Because of his deep-seated feelings of mistrust and shame at the deprived conditions fate had thrust upon his family, he had grown ever more introverted. His only friends were the sufferings of his youth. His nervous appearance, weak frame, and indifferent health were matters of grave concern to him. But still, his dreams remained towering and unwavering.'

'He got his first job after matriculation as a salesman with a local distributor of Pakistan Tobacco Company. He continued trying to supplement his income with minor jobs in textile mills and other factories under harsh working conditions. But his resolve to accomplish big goals landed him in a college.

Persistently following the path of his dreams, he never let discouragement or depression overcome him. To everyone's surprise, he succeeded in winning two gold medals both in the Intermediate and in his Bachelor's.'

The pin-drop silence at the Dubai expo center was broken by the ringing echoes of applause from the audience, all of whom were thoroughly spellbound by the story.

'His obsession with achieving something significant for his family had made him restless. He found it intolerable to wait for admission to the university for a whole long year. He left his village and headed for Lahore, where he embarked on a struggling life that would challenge every ounce of grit in him. Not willing to waste even a single day, he began to learn computer hardware at Hafeez Centre during the mornings and worked at the Jang newspaper canteen in the evenings. His life was characterized by hunger, homelessness, and other similar problems.

'But with God's grace, he won admission to the M. Sc. at Punjab University. Meanwhile, he worked full-time as a translator at a magazine. He wanted to start his professional life as soon as possible, but he was destined for yet further adversity. During his very first year at university, his father departed this world, leaving him to face life's challenges all alone.

His father was indeed his best friend, his companion, his source of inspiration, and his reason to accomplish something big in life.

He was totally devastated and depressed by his father's death. Without the will to go on, for a while, he seriously considered ending his life. His heart filled with grief, he did not see any hope, any purpose, any reason to live and continue his struggle for success. However, his family and friends rallied around and provided him much-needed support. Finally, he decided to reconnect with his lofty dreams and return to the pursuit of his goals.

He resumed his struggle for success. However, all kinds of emotional, financial, social, mental, physical, and psychological challenges blocked his path. It seemed like life was really determined to test his courage, nerve, and determination to the limit.

'During his last year at university, he was fortunate to find a mentor who took him in hand, challenged his beliefs and, guided him to set clear goals. He inspired him to study the books that stirred, inspired, and motivated him, and exceptionally stimulated his life and intellect.

'When he completed his M. Sc., his family was impatiently waiting to reap the rewards of his success. But they had no idea that he was still being pursued by other demons, the victim of other defeats. He was unemployed and thus had no money to fulfill the promises he had made to his family.

He used to get up every morning, see the job ads in newspapers, apply for the jobs, appear in interviews only to get rejected.

He failed in over 250 job interviews, a handful of them for the position of a waiter in five start hotels. No company was willing to give him a chance even without a salary. Indeed he had nothing to show in terms of both personality and skills to justify his ambition.

A little later, he joined the visiting faculty of M.A.O. College Lahore and started teaching M. Sc. classes. However, his monthly salary was less than US$18. His dream appeared destined to remain unfulfilled.

'He continued his struggle to create a meaningful life for himself, but nothing seemed to go in his favor. He knocked on dozens of doors, from ordinary street academies to the Civil Services Academy. Still, nobody was willing to offer him anything. Punjab University and the Pakistan Air Force rejected him twice. He also got turned down by the Public Service Commission, leaving him depressed and disillusioned. However, he was still unwilling to let go of his glorious dreams. But he was not ready to give up.

He decided to once again appear for the Public Service Commission exam. And this time, he passed, and also conquered the *first position in the Public Service Commission*. Though his heart pulled him to pursue his real passions, his family needed financial security. So he was forced to join the government service. He became a lecturer at a Government Degree College Baseerpur in District Okara, but his dreams kept him restless.

'One lesson he had learned well from his gurus was that you cannot venture into uncharted waters unless you say goodbye to the shoreline.

'Finally, he mustered up the courage to bid goodbye to a college lectureship that was earning him $ 60 a month for his family. Annoying almost everyone, he decided to return to Lahore and refocused on his most desired dream to build a company. He wanted to become an entrepreneur and make a difference in the world by helping individuals and organizations achieve greatness.

His vision to set up a company was almost thrashed by hundreds of obstacles. No money, no references, no resources, no social or professional network, no experience, no transport, no clients, no food, no equipment, no computer, no printer, no laptop, no cell phone, and even no place to live. And worst of all, no place to live. The toughest decision at the end of every day was where to spend the night? But his courage remained undaunted, and his dreams unwavering.

'He took his cutting-edge ideas on transforming businesses to dozens of companies and organizations but came away disappointed. From hospitals to one-room clinics, he left no stone unturned, but his efforts were no avail. The toughest dilemma he had to struggle with was that none of his family members believed in him. The people dearest to him started making negative comments about his character. Their predictions about his future were far from flattering.

'He had no permanent place to live in Lahore. He did have some relatives, but he did not feel comfortable staying with them. Friends were not ready to tolerate him for long, except for a few outstanding ones, most of whom were going through the same rough time. The constant shifting of homes left him frustrated and cost him dozens of his favorite books and the clothes he had bought with his brow's sweat. His siblings were beginning to insist that he return to his native town as he was unemployed and, according to them, 'hopeless.'

'He tried his luck with countless people and launched numerous initiatives, but it began to seem as if circumstances were conspiring against him. He gave the impression of being very motivated and with a burning desire to do something bigger to those around him. Still, deep down in his heart, he was almost ready to throw in the towel. But every time he came close to the end, something inside him kept him going.'

'Finally, he found an office where he could invite his clients. It was not less than McDonald's LDA branch. (Actually, he just pretended to himself that this was his office though he had no address printed on his business card.) He started visiting McDonald's every day, mostly on foot, as he could not afford even public transport. His potential clients would come to meet him at McDonald's. During those two-and-a-half financially strapped years, he NEVER ate a McDonald's burger – simply because he couldn't afford one. He would offer his clients only a cup of tea or a cone ice cream, and if a client asked why he was not having one himself, he would say airily, 'Oh, I just had some.'

'Ignoring his acute hunger pangs, he would continue reading, writing, researching, and preparing his proposals for clients. He had redirected his hunger towards a bigger purpose. If his hunger became unbearable, he would have a bite to eat at some small, cheap roadside food stall and then return to McDonald's to continue his work. In one of the noisiest, most crowded and distracting venues, McDonald's, not only did he meet his clients, prepare for his assignments, carry out research projects, set the direction of his life, orchestrated plans, dreamt big dreams to set up a great company; but he also managed to write his masterpiece *Tick Tick Dollar*™.'

The hall was filled with an electric silence.

'Now, have you figured out how I know this boy so well?' the speaker asked in a quivering, almost tearful tone of voice, 'Because he is no one else but me – Qaiser Abbas!'

Every person in the hall completely stunned, emotionally charged, stood up and applauded him with eyes wet and unshed tears. The audience left their seats and gathered around him on the stage. Everyone had tears in their eyes.

The unstoppable applause was deafening. The high-profile corporate executives from over 100 countries were deeply touched, inspired, and shaken up. They were showering their love on him by hugging even kissing him.

My friend Qaiser Abbas was touched by this first standing ovation given to him by the 1500 enthusiastic global leaders in the audience that his emotions overcame him. He started crying like the child he once was. He found it difficult to believe that his dreams were actually coming true.

He wanted everyone to know from his own experience that nothing in this world can keep people from fulfilling their most precious, seemingly impossible dreams. Turning back to the audience, he said in a voice ringing with emotion, 'starting from nothing, if I can stand here today; if you commit 100% to your dreams, where can you reach?'

I can assure you that Qaiser Abbas is undoubtedly living the life of his dreams today. During his motivational speech in Muscat, addressing over 100 CEOs organized by WJ Towell Group, Qaiser received multiple standing ovations. When he finished, people could not think of any better way to demonstrate their appreciation for touching their hearts and minds. They gave him one new, unique tribute by standing on their chairs and applauding.

World's #1 Leadership Coach, Dr. Marshall Goldsmith, has endorsed Qaiser's 'Dare Coaching Framework'™. He is the Master Mind behind one of the fastest-growing Coach-Networks, spread in four continents with over 250 Certified Coaches.

In his 20 years journey as Leadership Coach, Qaiser has had the privilege to coach CEOs, business leaders, celebrities and superstars of sports, movies, and media. His ceaseless pursuit of excellence and the sharing of his inspiration place him as one of the top global motivational speakers.

His clients include many Fortune 500 companies like Toyota, GE, Nestle, Philips, Total, Schlumberger, Coca Cola, PepsiCo, Unilever, Abbott, and Reckitt-Benckiser.

Qaiser is the recipient of the 'Brian Tracy International Excellence Award 2017, held in London. During this award ceremony, he shared stage with the legend Brian Tracy in the presence of 6000 people from 70 different countries. He is also the recipient of the 'Trainer of the Year' Award for Asia by the World HRD Congress, Singapore.

Qaiser's is on a mission to instill self-belief, hope, and the certainty of an abundant success for everyone, especially the youth of Pakistan.

From beginnings of despair and hopelessness, with no resources, money, or capital at all, Qaiser won through to found one of the most innovative Management Development & Consulting companies, *Possibilities*, now operating in 40 countries. He chose for himself the title of *Chief Inspiring Officer* rather than the more traditional Chief Executive Officer.

> Qaiser's purpose in life is to: Inspire, educate, and empower people to passionately live a purposeful life, filled with achievement and fulfillment.

To him, the purpose is not about getting, it is about giving. Why? Because when you focus on giving, God liberates you from the pursuit of getting.

Qaiser is also the Founder of the Possibilities Foundation, aiming to establish non-formal Possibilities Schools to educate underprivileged children of Pakistan. Once his dream was to be able to sponsor one child to the kind of school where he couldn't afford to go as a child. Today, he supports hundreds of deprived kids to study in a school of their own choice—all through his personal income.

Qaiser's 100% income from his books and a significant portion of his speaking fee is dedicated to supporting his back-to-society initiatives.

Join Qaiser Abbas in his pursuit of *possibilitizing dreams* for everyone to learn, share, and grow, especially for those who are less privileged, deprived, and forgotten.

THE CORE PHILOSOPHY
TICK TICK DOLLAR™

If you dare to face your fears and design a purposeful life filled with success, prosperity, and fulfillment, this book is my gift. The purpose of my life is to help people do, share, give, and create what they possibly can and build a meaningful life along the way.

In this book, I am going to give you two gifts:

1. The gift of my philosophy on living a great life grounded in values, fulfillment, and passion
2. And the gift of 14 proven principles offering practical tools, insights, and strategies to translate your life vision into reality.

I have been studying peak performance for the past 14 years. I have committedly devoted fourteen years of my life to discover the principles that can help you live the life you always desired. But the most important thing that I am going to share with you in this book is the gift of my philosophy encompassing three life-saving words – purpose, passion, and performance. The right alignment of these magic words can turn your life around as they did for me. And I mean it.

THE PURPOSELESS PURSUIT

Over the last fourteen years, I have worked as a Success Coach with top business leaders, relentless entrepreneurs, exceptionally gifted CEOs, superstars of movies, champion athletes, award-winning actors, sought-after writers, veteran media giants, stunning supermodels, best-selling authors, most elegant television anchors, crowed pulling singers & musicians, genius army generals, and prize-winning scientists.

It is my great privilege to help these superstars learn, practice, and live & breathe the same philosophy and principles you will be learning in this book.

It was quite shocking to see that despite being at the top of their games, some of these super achievers were inwardly empty, broken, and unfulfilled. The fame, money, status, and power they had gained over the years they had paid a heavy price, were no longer satisfying. In most private and heart to heart discussions with me, they confessed that they indeed were in deep pain.

Based on their situation, I can quickly put them into three categories:

Category #01:

Category one includes people who are relentlessly following their passion with some degree of success without a clear sense of purpose. They never thought of the need to know why they do what they do? What is their real reason for being in this role? They hardly tried to find out why they are here and why those unique talents and skills were gifted to them in the first place.

Category #02:

In the second group are the ones who have a sense of purpose. That means they know what their direction should be but have no clue what their true passion is. They don't know how to change course and which path to follow to get closer to their reason for existing.

Category #03:

The third kind is those who know both their purpose and passion. But somehow have not found a way to link them both together. Their purpose pulls them in the north, but the passion is in the south. Hence they have never been able to leverage their gifts to be what they could have been. They live a mediocre life and never get to realize their full potential. Also, they experience a distinct sense of dissatisfaction from life.

In my one-on-one coaching sessions with them, I share the gift of Tick Tick Dollar philosophy. They learn to build a sense of alignment between them and what they love to do. Once they can see the connection between their purpose and passion, their performance skyrockets, they are ready to take charge, make better choices, and gain the strength from what they have previously perceived as suffering.

THE DISCOVERY

Tick Tick Dollar philosophy is not my invention; it is my discovery. I discovered this philosophy when I was at the lowest point in my own life. I had tried everything I read in self-help books, but nothing changed.

My 24 years struggle to turn my life around brought me to a point where I was homeless, jobless, visionless, hopeless, resourceless, loveless, and almost lifeless. My annual income was less than 200$.

I had a destructive self-image, stumpy self-confidence, and a weak concept about who I was and what I thought I could do. I had lost faith and was nearly about to give up. And then I embraced Tick Tick Dollar philosophy.

This philosophy has been my inspiration and guiding star to live a life that a mere couple of years ago would have seemed unthinkable even in my remotest imaginations. Today, this unbelievably blessed life is a reality.

From humble beginnings, making $ 18 a month, and establishing a global management development & consulting group (*Possibilities*), Tick Tick Dollar™ philosophy has been my guide every step.

It empowered me to manage a successful business, serving over 500 clients, including many Fortune 500 companies and governments. Possibilities Group is also running two heart-warmingly positive contributions to social projects. One is Possibilities Foundation, and the other is Possibilities Schools, offering free education to thousands of underprivileged children.

> It doesn't matter whether you are already a superstar or feel lost like I was a few years ago; this philosophy has the power to change your life. It is a *tried and true* recipe for creating the life you desire for yourself.

This seems to be a big claim. And who do you think will confirm the authenticity of my claim? At the very least, those closely associated with me who knew me when I was practically on the street, without food in my belly, broken both financially and emotionally. They all knew me as someone who was disheartened, fearful, shy, disappointed, lost, and nervous.

They can undoubtedly recognize me as someone whose personality, appearance, presence, grooming, conversation, and presentation never matched his aspirations, big ideas, philosophy, and dreams.

Some of these verifiers are my creditors, to whom I often failed to pay back the money I borrowed from them! My teachers, students, clients, relatives, friends, and family members, most of whom did not believe in me, would be willing to take the stand to support my statement.

Everybody thought I was destined to fail, spoil my life, and never accomplish anything worthwhile. Indeed, most of them suggested me to stop wasting time chasing my dreams and start worrying about bringing food to the table for the family.

In those life-threatening moments, this philosophy kept me alive, determined, and motivated when there were no substantial reasons to back it up. There is a considerable list of my current clients willing to validate this philosophy.

A few years ago, these clients were not ready to give me a shot even when I offered my services unconditionally free of cost. They were right. At that time, of course, as I had no experience or track record to back up my fire, passion, and enthusiasm.

THE DREAMS

Tick Tick Dollar™ *approach* was my companion, my inspiration, and my north star in all those frustrating, shattering, and devastating instants. The fact is that with no financial resources, no professional network, no background, and no *confidence*, God granted me all that which a few years ago existed only in my imagination. Let me share some of my dreams (not the goals) on my list in those days:

Wearing made-to-measure clothes, eating a fancy meal, having my own personal computer, buying a cell phone, having shoes of my own size, flying in an airplane, staying at a five-star hotel, driving my own car, buying a Walkman, supporting my under-privileged family, sending a needy child to the best school in town, making two hundred dollars a month, opening my bank account, playing golf, learning to swim, visiting a big city, appearing on TV, living in an up-market home, meeting my favorite celebrities, adventuring with rock climbing, walking on a beach, conducting training sessions in the mountains, being able to address large audiences, having my hair cut at a fancy salon, writing and publishing best-selling books, becoming an international motivational speaker, achieving financial freedom, establishing myself as the premium Success Coach, travelling internationally, making a significant contribution to society, and reaching 764 other similar hopes, dreams and ambitions that I *believed* at that time to be *completely unrealistic* became a concrete reality for me.

My entire being is filled with a deep sense of gratitude to the Almighty that what I had always considered being far-fetched and incredible visions of success turned into actuality.

Imagine for a moment that a young man who didn't dare even introduce himself to another person in the corporate world because he lacked self-esteem and confidence is now inspiring millions through his speaking engagements.

He teaches leaders how to break their self-imposed limits, faces their brutal fears, and mark a difference by recognizing their gifts. A courage-less professional, whose constant habit was fleeing away *instead of seizing the opportunities*, finally musters the nerve to stand tall *as an alternative to escaping* and facing the challenge of speaking to a variety of groups ranging from 8 to 8000 in his motivational programs.

What made me do all of this that I could never have imagined doing even in my daydreams only a few short years ago? It was just a simple shift in my thinking, beliefs, and philosophy. I committed myself to stick to three decisions I made at a time when my life was in a complete directionless mess.

1. Each day I will commit to following my purpose
2. I will use every waking moment to pursue my most profound passion
3. Every day, I will use the joint power of my purpose and passion for performing at the most exceptional optimum levels.

THE QUEST OF ALIGNMENT

The gift of my philosophy takes you way beyond the traditional peak performance or success tools. It essentially is a mindset that challenges you to listen to your inner calling, redirect your enormous potential to move toward it, and live gracefully with an unquestionable legacy.

This book elaborates on the same philosophy for you that turned my own life around. It will guide and inspire you to live with purpose and passion and achieve a superior performance every day.

The best thing this book can give you is the genius of building alignment between your reason for existence, what you really feel passionate about, and how you can make a conscious commitment to perform at the optimum levels that others can only desire.

The right configuration, alliance, and union between *purpose, passion,* and *performance* will bring a more profound sense of joy, satisfaction, and fulfillment. It will guarantee goal achievement, balanced living, fulfillment, and a profound sense of accomplishment.

You will embark on a journey that gives free rein to your true potential. Your daily stresses, worries, and anxieties will be transformed into your allies to help you achieve breakthrough performances in significant areas of your life. You will move away from excuses and start orchestrating positive changes in your life.

You will get rid of the justifications, explanations, and rationalizations that have reinforced your unspoken belief that you are mediocre. You will stop *apologizing* and will start living the life that is out there waiting for you.

Tick Tick Dollar™ will introduce a renewed sense of achievement and fulfillment by focusing on what has real value. You will realize the importance and feel the urge to make better decisions while taking full charge of the results.

Your mind will begin to experience freedom from irritating disturbances and achieve greater calm, serenity, and peace. The new choices will allow you to pick a healthier, happier, and more prosperous life.

The complete Tick Tick Dollar™ philosophy is explained in a nutshell below:

- First tick is a reminder for you to *live on purpose*
- Second tick prompts you to *live your passion*
- Dollar challenges you to *outperform* opposition in pursuit of your purpose and passion.

The day I committed to doing my very best to live this philosophy every day, it proved to be the turning point of my life. For many years, I never believed in my own story. I had no idea that a gift of speaking and inspiring others in waiting to be unleashed inside me. I never thought that talking about my pains will bring healing, inspiration, and motivation for others.

I discovered the truth that purpose is who you are, and passion is what you do. When who you are is aligned with what you do; you become unstoppable. When I built the alignment between my purpose and passion, my life began to experience a new level of excitement.

Though I had no money, I was happy. I was resource-less but satisfied. I was on the street but fulfilled inside. I knew for sure that my Creator had touched my heart for a reason. I knew He has some plans for me, far better and trustworthy than the ones I had for myself.

My purpose gave me the power to spread positivity, hope, and inspiration to the world. The power of purpose enabled me to overcome my fears, anxieties, and negativities. The sense of purpose ignited within me my buried passion for public speaking. Soon, I could see my unstoppable passion for delivering a pro-life, pro-success, pro-dreams, and pro-hope message.

I urge you to begin your quest to discover your purpose and passion today. Whichever you find first, make sure that you make both aligned when you see the second one. If you find your purpose first, find the most passionate way to pursue it. If you find your passion first, catch a way to use it to serve others, and praise the Creator, you will automatically detect your purpose.

Remember, living every day with purpose and passion for optimum performance guarantees achievement and fulfillment.

Only a 100% commitment to maximizing your purpose, passion, and performance certifies success and prosperity. Starting from today, 'Living your purpose and passion for optimum performance' must become the slogan of your life.

Are you ready to commit to living every day outperforming competing forces in pursuit of your purpose and passion?

PURPOSE

PURPOSE
FIND YOUR COMPASS

'To live your life's purpose means doing what you love to do, doing what you're good at, and accomplishing what's important to you.'
- Jack Canfield, Author of Chicken Soup for the Soul

Each one of us is unique. So is our purpose.

You are tailor-made for your purpose. If someone else was meant to accomplish *your* purpose, then there was no need for you to be in this world.

Your very existence on this planet is an indication that some purpose does exist for you. You and your purpose are supposed to co-exist. Your purpose and you are part of the same story, same journey, and same destination. You must make a conscious effort to find the other part of your story. And if you are still alive, it means the job you were sent to complete is still unfinished.

So what are you here for? Ignoring this question is not the solution. Choosing to sleepwalk through life without knowing why you are here is criminal. Every *tick* of the clock is basically a reminder to you to *live your life on purpose.*

The purpose is the answer to the question of why are you here, what are you here for, what is your agenda for landing at this planet, what is your reason for existence, and what is it that you are here to accomplish?

THE COMPASS

The best metaphor for explaining purpose is a 'compass'. Like a compass, your purpose gives you a sense of direction. The compass is a blessing for the lost travellers. Similarly, the purpose is a blessing for those who are off their path and feel lost.

Let me ask you a couple of questions to know whether or not you have a clear sense of purpose in life.

Do you accurately understand the meaning of your life?

Do you think there is something in your life that is so important to you that you can give up everything for that?

Can you clearly see how well you play your part to improve the lives of people on this planet?

How and where do you think you can leave your mark?

Have you ever thought about the way you would like to be remembered?

Did you ever try listening to your life's calling? Or are you still waiting?

Most of us struggle to find the answers to these questions. We are so busy chasing a life that we fail to find time to reflect on the meaning and purpose of our existence on this planet. Who brought us here, and what does He want us to do for HIM? It never occurs to most of us to devote some quality time to find answers to the most critical questions of our life.

If you are one of those who feel lost, don't worry. It is pretty standard. I have been lost for good 24 years as well. However, my experience is, when you are ready to change course, you get unexpected magical support.

The best beginning would be to start finding ways to serve others wherever you possibly can. Because when we choose to help others, purpose invariably finds us.

WHY PURPOSE?

'Know what success really means to you. Find out what it is that brings true meaning to your life. What makes each day important for you and then focus on it.'- Warren Buffett

Why live on purpose? Because having a sense of purpose and heading toward it gives you a feeling of direction. You *know* deep inside that you are accomplishing something significant and getting to a meaningful place.

Purpose gives you a reason to get out of bed with a smile every morning and look forward to what the day will bring. Also, it gives you a yardstick to measure the distance between where you are and where you are destined to be.

A life lived with purpose gives you confidence, a sense of triumph, and a feeling of gratification. Purpose puts a bounce in your step and ensures you a mind full of vigor. When you decide to live your purpose, it gives you a direction to navigate more forcefully through the turbulent waters.

Purpose reinforces your will to handle challenges, solve problems, manage turmoil, and bounce back from setbacks to continue what you are meant to accomplish.

GOAL VS. PURPSOE – DIFFERNCE

The goal and *purpose, usually* are interchangeably used. Nonetheless, to me, purpose and goal are two different creatures. They are two banks of the same canal. Let's explore the critical distinctions between the two most important concepts. If you wish to create a great life, the following points will help you a great deal.

Time:

The goal has a definite starting and finishing line. However, the purpose is a never-ending quest. One purpose can accommodate multiple goals with many beginnings and ends.

Completion:

A goal can be achieved with dedicated effort. Yet, no matter how much effort you put in to pursue your purpose, it will never be fully realized. Shocked? If you are following the real purpose, your whole life will be consumed in pursuit of your purpose, yet you will still believe there is a lot still undone.

Joy:

The satisfaction and pleasure you experience upon achieving a goal are short-lived. You may temporarily feel the sense of fun, but soon the feeling of pleasure fades. However, even if you accomplish the tiniest portion of your purpose, the joy and satisfaction you experience are lasting, durable, and eternal.

Value:

The goal, if achieved, produces value for you only. Purpose, when completed, generates tremendous value, benefits, and advantages to others.

Focus:

While chasing a goal, you glorify yourself and ignore people. But when you pursue a purpose, you glorify God and serve people.

Impact:

The effect of achieving a goal usually is short term. Conversely, the realization of a purpose has long term lifelong effects on generations to come.

Feeling:

Reaching a goal gives you a sense of achievement. Attaining a purpose provides you a taste of fulfillment.

Direction:

Goal urges you to *get* as much as you can, whereas purpose inspires you to *give* as much as you can.

KEY POINT:

A tiny shift in direction can turn a goal into purpose. And that small shift is re-thinking the reasons for undertaking any goal. If you build intent to serve others through the same goal and withdraw from the desire to serve yourself, it automatically earns the credentials to be titled as a purpose.

CONVERTING GOAL INTO PURPOSE

'I truly believe that everything that we do and everyone that we meet is put in our path for a purpose. There are no accidents; we're all teachers - if we're willing to pay attention to the lessons we learn, trust our positive instincts and not be afraid to take risks or wait for some miracle to come knocking at our door.'
- Marla Gibbs

I have three good news for you.

1. You have the power and guts to pursue your bigger purpose of life
2. At the same time, every single moment, you have the opportunity to bring purposefulness in everything you do on a day to day basis.
3. Also, you can build alignment between whatever you do to the overall reason for your being.

Once you make a decision to live *on purpose,* the invigorating sense of purpose will be reflected in almost every action of yours.

For instance, you set out to make a presentation to a very high-profile audience. If you have *goal-driven,* self-serving thinking, you will feel the pressure. The stress will exhaust you. You know why? Because you need the audience to like you, admire you, appreciate your work, approve your idea, or do business with you. Since what you need is in their hand and you are not sure whether they will give you what you need as a 'taker', you will feel anxiety, nervousness, and worry. This goal-centered thinking will be reflected through your words, body language, and actions.

On the other hand, if you are purpose-centric, you arrive at the place as a 'giver'. You let your sense of purpose guide your thoughts and behavior. Your focus is shifted from what you can *get* to what you can *give*. You are doing your best so that your presentation can *serve* them the best.

> Instead of worrying about yourself, you are focused on giving participants a feeling of comfort, confidence, and relaxation. You are committed to *providing* them the best return on the time they have invested in attending your presentation.

You promise to help them and offer them more value. You commit to contributing, trying your best to reduce some of their anxieties, pressures, and concerns. You focus on finding ways so that your presentation can bring about a positive change in their lives.

What is happening here? You have shifted your focus from *your needs* (what you want) to *their needs (what do they want)*. *Their* needs and wishes have become the focal point of your efforts. Your objective is no more to win their approval, admiration, or appreciation. You are not going there to *get* something; you are going there to *give*.

The shift in thinking will shift the center of your energies. Instead of worrying about the presentation, you will organize your material in a way that excites your audience. Givers feel no pressure. They move their attention away from the outcome and put the spotlight on the purpose.

When participants see the value in your work and get what they want, you are actually increasing your chances of getting what you want? When you focus on giving, you automatically get what you want.

In a nutshell, if you aim to do something that will bring *benefit to you*, you chase a goal. When you do the same thing so that *others can benefit*, you bring purpose in the picture. A goal is about *getting*, whereas purpose is about *giving*. Here is some food for thought for all those who wish to create a successful and prosperous future for them.

'The world gives to the givers and takes from the takers.'

Start performing your duties with a reason to facilitate and support others. Your aim should be to helps others shine, to kindle their growth and improve their quality of life. By doing so, each moment of your life will be consumed in pursuit of your purpose. This will automatically adjust *your* own quality of life.

Success begins when you convert a goal into a purpose.

Ask yourself: *'What can I do to discover the purpose God has created me to accomplish right now?'*

TEST OF PURPOSE

The simplest definition of purpose is *'giving'*. Wherever you are right now and whatever you are doing at the moment, stop doing it and ask yourself this simple question: Is my intent here to give or get? Do I intend to give or get?

The shortest test of whether or not someone is following purpose is this:

Who is this act serving, you or others? If it is serving you only, it's not purpose-based. If it is helping others, it surely is.

How does 'giving' figure in this? It means evaluating the deep-down *intentions and reasons* behind your decisions to carry out the projects, schemes, and ventures in your life.

If your sole intent behind doing something is to secure benefits, rewards, and prizes for your own self, this is *not* the purpose. If the focus is only on *getting*, your endeavors lack a sense of purpose. However, if you are doing it to *'give,'* that undoubtedly is purpose-driven.

Can you see the very small, but distinct difference of intent here? When embarking on a job, if you focus only on what you are getting out of it, you will make no progress. On the other hand, if your focus is on how you can contribute more, and use this as an opportunity to bring value and benefit to others, you are not only getting closer to a meaningful purpose, you are also sowing the seeds of enduring success for yourself.

FINDING YOUR PURPOSE

The journey to discover your life's purpose helps you discern your deepest motivations and brings greater clarity and focus to every day and every facet of your life. It inspires you to be all that you can be and to live an ever more vibrant, fuller life. To explore this in detail, read Dr. Wayne Dyer's *The Power of Intention,* a profoundly inspiring book intended to awaken you to your full potential. Discovering your purpose will take some effort on your part, but the return on your investment will be tremendous.

The process of living your purpose starts with knowing what your purpose is. I am sharing with you a simple set of questions to probe into it:

STEP 01:

Choose a group or segment of society that you feel excited about serving.

STEP 02:

How do you want their lives to be changed? How will you impact their lives by serving them? What will they be able to accomplish?

STEP 03:

What specific talent, ability, and skill you will be using to make it happen for them? How would you make it possible?

LIVING ON PURPOSE

There is no shortcut to living a purposeful life. Below is the step by step process you must follow to make sure that you are connected with your purpose.

1. **Listen:**
   Show willingness and commitment to listen to your inner calling. You will have to stop listening to everyone else and pay complete attention to what your deep voice is trying to tell you.

2. **Verify:**
   Make sure that the call you are responding to is the real one, not a false alarm. Many people spend a lot of time trailing a purpose and then changing the path, realizing it was not something coming from the core of their heart. They mistakenly took that 'fake' call as real.

3. **Follow:**
   Take immediate action to begin the journey of following the path. Tracking the way will require energy, patience, and full devotion.

4. **Familiarize:**
   Develop a trusting relationship with your purpose, making your purpose your most important partner.

5. **Flight:**
The expedition to follow your purpose is not a part-time job. It is a full-time commitment. It's binding to consistently move toward it with speed, accuracy, and sense of urgency.

6. **Line-up:**
Once you take off for 'purpose flight', all your attitudes, behaviors, abilities, skills, competencies, and capacities should be aligned in the same direction.

7. **Review:**
Periodically take time out to see how much distance you have already covered. What significant milestones are waiting ahead? Review your progress on a regular basis. And don't forget to celebrate small victories.

ACTIONS:

1. Find your overall purpose of life
2. Develop a sense of purpose in anything you do in life
3. Make every moment a reflection of purpose-based living

Tick Tick Dollar is a wake-up call to connect with your compass! (Purpose). It is never too late to find your purpose.

> The purpose of human life is to serve and to show compassion and the will to help others. - Albert Schweitzer

PASSION

PASSION
CONNECT TO YOUR HEART

Passion is the reservoir that fuels your purpose. Passion is a pool of vigor to guarantee unwavering movement toward your purpose despite obstacles and disappointments. Passion keeps you lively and animated by providing the positive energy you require to face life's toughest challenges. It will give you the strength and motivation to do the work you need to do to head in the direction you most want.

When you are passionate, you will experience no difficulty waking up in the morning and pursuing the things that bring you closer to your purpose. There could be a dozen other things you would like to do, but when you are passionate about something, you care more deeply about it, plan it, and set specific goals to accomplish it.

Without passion, nothing brings significant or unusual results. All successful people are so passionate about what they do that they probably cannot conceive any other way of living. Passion energizes them to create outstanding results in their respective fields. They view their job, profession, or business as an *obsession*. That is why they consistently outperform others in their areas. This fascination gives them the drive and motivation that keeps them going every time, all the time.

THE HEART

> *"Follow your happiness. Even if you don't end up making a fortune, you'll at least be doing what you love.'*
> Mark Zuckerberg, CEO, Facebook

The most excellent metaphor for passion is the 'heart'.

The heart represents Love, the most powerful emotion a human being can ever experience. So does the passion. Passion is close to your heart. Your passion secures an exceptional place in your heart. When you pursue your true passion, your heart is filled with joy, pleasure, and bliss.

Imagine the delight of finding your true Love. That's the exact charm you feel when you find your true passion. The time you spend with your true passion (Love) becomes the most precious treasure of your life.

SIGNS OF LOVE (PASSION)

> *"Love is the spiritual essence of what we do. The technique is the manifestation of the preparation and investment as a result of Love."*
> Wynton Marsalis, To a Young Jazz Musician

Sign # 01: **Obsession**

When your heart is filled with Love, you almost feel obsessed with talking about it. You want a good pair of ears that can listen to your *stories.* Similarly, passionate people are almost fixated to talk about their *Love* – the upcoming project, movie, painting, book, or whatever they are working on. They grab every opportunity to speak about what they truly feel passionate about.

Sign # 02: **Commitment**

True Love requires commitment. All passionate people are known for their commitment. The exactly know how to keep going even when the going gets tough. Their level of commitment is unquestionable. They are not ready to give up, no matter what. Their sense of commitment gives them a renewed sense of energy, vitality, and confidence to keep moving in their passion.

Sign # 03: **Focus**

No matter where you are and what you do, your Love neither likes nor allows you to dedicate focus to anything else. Likewise, your passion forces you to keep you absorbed in the activities bringing you closer to your passion.

Sign # 04: **Risk**

Love is the best teacher to help you master the art of risk-taking. When you are in Love, you are far more prone to take risks you otherwise cannot even think of taking. So is the case with passionate people. Passion inspires you to be bold, face your fears, and do whatever it takes to unleash your passion.

Sign # 05: **Stretch**

Love gives you the power to break your limits and go beyond the barriers. People in Love are not impressed with fences. They are not afraid of railings. By the same token, passionate people are not scared by walls, frightened by obstacles, alarmed by borders, or horrified by hedges. They are masters of broadening thinking and stretching actions to match the challenge ahead.

HOW TO DISCOVER YOUR PASSION?

'Inside each and every one of us is one, true authentic swing, something he was born with. Something that is ours, and ours alone, something that can't be taught to you, or learned, something that got to be remembered. Over time, the world can rob us of that swing, and it can get buried under all our would-haves, and could- have, and should-haves. Some folk even forget what their swing was like.'
- Will Smith in The Legend of Bagger Vance

Like lost Love, many of us have a lost passion. To help you get a grip on discovering your (lost) passion, let me share five proven strategies to help you detect your passion.

If you are sincere and entirely determined, you will definitely allocate some time to find the answers to these questions raised in each strategy. The easiest thing is to skip the step and continue to follow the guesswork or the false alarms taking you nowhere. I suggest you invest serious time to explore what you are naturally inclined to and are reasonably good at doing it.

Ready? Here are those no-fail strategies for you.

Strategy #01:

Remember the days when you woke up in the morning, and you were totally excited, enthused, and energetic because you were looking forward to something. What was that? What was different about those days? What made you so excited about those days? What were you anticipating? What was pulling you towards?

Strategy #02:

Imagine you have all the money in the word, and starting from today, you will never have to worry again for making money. What would you be doing starting from today?

Strategy #03:

Do you have any special skills that you think are purely God gifted? When you perform one of those activities, you don't feel like putting in any energy. It is almost effortless. People around you feel surprised because it is complicated, though, and impossible to master the skill at this level.

Strategy #04:

Is there anything in your life you love doing so much that you are willing to do it free, without expecting to get the money?

You are ready to do free for pure Love, not for money; that's precisely the work world will be ready to pay you for hugely.

Strategy #05:

Have you ever thought of getting retired? What is it you would love to do when you get retired? Why wait for retirement? Why don't you start doing it now? Why postpone your passion till retirement? What if you convert this passion into a profession now and never get retired!

If you still struggle to determine how you will mark a difference in this world, the best starting point would be to identify where your talents and skills are residing? If you found this 'life-work' difficult, you will quickly be changing courses. You might have already changed some courses (jobs and professions, etc.), expecting to find your true passion.

Remember, finding your passion is not an accident; it requires constant digging, plowing, mining, and tunnelling. You will have to make a deliberate effort to begin the quest to discover what your life is all about.

YOUR PASSION CATALOGUE

Let's build an inventory of things you *feel* passionate about. Don't ignore any activity. You may even include the activities you have never done before, but you wish to do them and feel excited about doing them. The list will emerge from the following:

- Your hobbies
- Activities that engage you
- Something you feel thrilled about doing
- Pastimes that excite you
- Actions that make you feel good

TEST – MY PASSION AWARD

'Your time is limited, so don't waste it living someone else's life. Don't be trapped by dogma — which is living with the results of other people's thinking. Don't let the noise of others' opinions drown out your own inner voice. And most important, dare to follow your heart and intuition. They somehow already know what you truly want to become. Everything else is secondary.'
– Steve Jobs [Stanford Speech 2005]

Your passion catalogue might have hundreds of items in it. However, for an item to be recognized as your true passion, it will have to go through three tests. You will only entitle it as 'My Passion' if it passes all three tests. Even if it fails one of these tests, it's gone. Disqualified for 'My Passion' title.

Test # 01: Test of Pull

Make a list of all the activities that you love doing so much that they regularly powerfully pull you. This pull is so strong that you want to say goodbye to everything else. You feel like releasing your breaks. You want to breakdown all the chains. You are always on the lookout to grab the chance. You instantly jump at every opportunity to perform that activity. You are almost dying to express that skill.

Test # 02: Test of Time

Of all the activities from test one, what engages you so much that you forget the sense of time. You feel so involved that hours pass by, and you don't even realize. Once you are engrossed in the act, time slows down. Days pass in minutes. Moreover, there are no signs of fatigue, boredom, or exhaustion.

You feel fresher at the end of the activity comparing to the beginning of the activity. You don't like to be interrupted in the middle. The world for you is non-existent. It is only you and the task you want to perform. You are obsessed, steadfast, and unstoppable.

Test # 03: Test of Feelings

This is the toughest test of all. I know many of your passions will pass the first two tests with ease. However, only a few will survive this stage and qualify for 'My Passion' award.

I understand you felt the pull to perform the act, and you lost the sense of time, too, because it was much engaging. However, the most crucial question is how you feel at the end of the activity. Does the activity leave you with a sense of gratification, satisfaction, and fulfillment? Or do you feel a sense of regret, remorse, or guilt?

If an activity that you pursue with passion doesn't leave you fulfilled is your *'directionless passion'*.

I found two reasons behind a directionless passion:

1. You have not been able to link your passion with a bigger purpose. You get up in the morning, you live your passion. However, your passion is not serving the world. The only measure of a fully directed passion is that it serves the world and people in it.
2. Your passion is misdirected. It contradicts the fundamental universal principles, values, and morals. For example, you are passionate about technology. However, you are passionately innovating a system to steal money from a bank. That won't give you fulfillment.

Any activity that makes you feel gratified, contented, and fulfilled when you finish doing it represents your true passion. Many people will find more than one activity matching the criteria. In that case, try to build intra-passion alignment too. If you love painting, reading, and mountaineering, find a way to connect the first and then direct them towards the purpose you are meant to pursue.

In case you remain uncertain about your real purpose and passion despite your best efforts, take a break. Instead of establishing a connection with your purpose, try establishing a connection with your Creator. Once you build this connection and become passionate about Him, He will surely guide you and reveal the path to you. All you have to do is show your commitment to do anything for Him.

When you devote yourself to a purpose that elevates Him, He will unquestionably lead you to the path that unlocks your potential and will make you the person He meant you to be.

ALIGNING PASSION WITH PURPOSE

'Find something you love to do so much, you can't wait for the sun to rise to do it all over again. The most inspiring leaders are those who don't work at a job, but pursue a calling.'
Chris Gardner, the real-life character of the movie
'The Pursuit of Happiness'. The once homeless man
turned multi-millionaire Stockbroker

Finding your passion is not enough. Without knowing what you are going to accomplish, using this passion will take you only that far. You must find a way to connect your passion with your purpose in life. Failing to do so will have two outcomes:

1. Your passion will only be half fulfilled. You will never realize your full potential
2. Some day when this passion fades, you will not know what to do with your life.

You need the energy to fulfill the purpose of your life. Where will this energy come from? What empowers you to stand tall against adversity at a time when moving even an inch appears impossible? The answer is passion.

The surest way to build a fulfilling life is to link your passion to your ultimate purpose in life and focus all your talents, abilities, and skills to realize it. When you discover your purpose in life and become absolutely passionate about it, you turn yourself into an unstoppable force. When others find reasons to 'lie-down-and-sleep'; your mantra in life becomes 'get-up-and-go'

Misalignment between your purpose and passion leads to frustration. With a sense of alignment, you will be better able to prioritize your passions and create a life that you will love. You will enjoy a life that works excellent for you and looks great to others to follow.

1. The purpose is the destination you want to reach. Passion is the vehicle that can get you there faster.
2. Purpose reveals to you the magical answer to the question, 'Why am I here?' Passion tells you the answer to another mystic question, 'What do I need to do to get there?'
3. The purpose is about 'what you want to give to this world'. Passion is about 'how will you make that possible'.
4. The purpose is your reason for existence. Once you correctly discover that reason, it doesn't change over time. However, your passions can change with time. You can use multiple passions to reach your purpose.
5. The purpose is your compass of life. Passion represents the heart. The real success in life comes to those who connect their compass with heart.

If you pursue your passion (and God gifted talents) to elevate yourself, you can still be very successful. However, your life will miss inner peace and a sense of joy. It means someday when your passion will dwindle for whatever reasons, your life will be meaningless, and you will feel the need to change your path.

Passion is a gift. It's your seed. One of my mentors, Dr. Wayne Dyer, once said to me that in every seed, there is hidden a *treeness*. Similarly, each one of us is a seed of greatness. That seed is our innate passion. As humans, our primary responsibility is to nurture this seed in us and use this gift to the fullest and create a purposeful life.

When we take personal responsibility to cultivate our distinctive gifts (passion), we create a life where our work and pleasure become one. If we continue to invest in cultivating our passion, it eventually does lead us to our ultimate purpose of life.

Keep in mind, don't foster your passion to only uplift yourself, secure position, feed your ego, or achieve status. Instead, use your passion to connect with people around you, uplift them, and touch the lives of those who meet you on this journey.

Unleash your passion for building a better world to whatever extent you can, inspiring as many lives as you can by the work you accomplish and leave your legacy that lasts beyond your lifetime.

WHY PEOPLE FAIL?

- They are unable to find their true passion
- They mistakenly follow the wrong passion
- They follow their passion for the wrong reason (feeding their own egos only)
- They keep following their directionless passion
- They fail to build alignment between various passions
- They fail to connect their passion with their purpose of life.

INSIGHTS:

1. Purpose and passion have to be totally aligned. That means they both must pull you in the same direction.
2. You can first discover your passion and find a purpose in pursuing and expressing it.
3. If you find your purpose first, then discover the most passionate ways to realize it.

Tick Tick Dollar is a wake-up call to connect your compass (purpose) with your heart (passion). It is never too late to pursue your passion.

'Do what you love. People with passion can change the world for the better. The passion I had for my work made all the difference.'
- Steve Jobs

PERFORMANCE

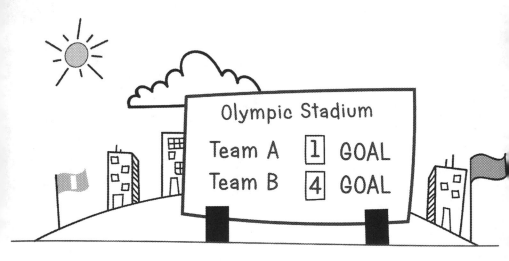

PERFORMANCE
SURPRISE THE SCOREBOARD

The highest performance levels come to people who are centered, intuitive, creative, and reflective - people who know to see a problem as an opportunity.
Deepak Chopra

We all want a remarkable life. However, our performance often falls short of our aspirations. How do you expect an extraordinary life to give you even a passing glance when your performance is unremarkable? How can you create first-rate success with a mediocre performance? How can you be a champion with below standard performance?

No matter how noble your life's purpose is and how committed you are to devote your passions to pursue it, your legacy will be short-lived if your *performance* is not impressive. To achieve great success, you cannot rely on average, commonplace, and routine performance. An ordinary performance will give you ordinary results, whereas a superb performance will bring you splendid rewards.

So what is the point I am making here? Very simple: to realize your purpose and passion, you will have to deliver an astonishing performance, time after time, and every time. Cheap and tasteless performance doesn't win any hearts. Only an outstanding performance can trigger a standing ovation.

You don't expect a disappointing, unsatisfactory, and substandard performance from a purpose-driven, passionate person. Whether it is a school, boardroom, or a sports stadium, no one is enthused by mediocrity. Everything is judged by performance.

If you don't meet the performance standards, you are just thrown out regardless of how passionate you are to play the game. People can neither touch your purpose nor feel your passion, but they see only your performance. It is your performance that reflects your passion and a sense of purpose.

What is the level of your current performance? If your performance is just run-of-the-mill, unremarkable, and underwhelming, success will continue to evade you.

PERFORMANCE & DOLLAR

Tick = Purpose
Tick = Passion
Dollar = Performance

There is no better than adversity. Every defeat, every heartbreak, every loss, contains its own seed, its own lesson on how to improve your performance the next time. - Malcolm X

Dollar in Tick Tick Dollar model represents all that comes with success, i.e., status, money, fame, lifestyle, prosperity, etc. Who doesn't like all of that? We all desire to possess all of those decorative items.

When you pay attention to the underlying message of two ticks of your life and achieve incredible performance pursuing your purpose and passion in the right spirit, the dollar begins to flow automatically. The dollars continue to shower on you like a never-ending rain until you shift your focus away from your purpose and stop pursuing your passion with the same intensity.

The core message here is that don't run after the money. Run after the purpose of using your passion. The money will run after you. The dollar is the applause from society for doing a remarkable job, making a difference, and uniquely touching people's lives. Anything that comes with the word dollar is the reward from your Creator for following His path and using His talents and skills to serve others.

Both achievement and fulfillment greet you at the success gate when you reach here following your purpose and passion. If you arrive at the success gate following any other path, the only achievement will greet you for a very brief period. You will never be able to see the face of fulfillment.

Fulfillment never resides in the hearts of those who remain disconnected from their purpose and passion.

THE SCORECARD

Confidence... thrives on honesty, on honor, on the sacredness of obligations, on faithful protection, and on unselfish performance. Without them, it cannot live. Franklin D. Roosevelt

The most obvious metaphor for performance is 'scoreboard.'

In the first two parts of the book, you have been listening to the softer stuff. This part of the book brings you the harder stuff. Like it or not, in this cut-throat, competitive, and fierce world, you will not be judged based on your private intentions but by your public performance.

People will not be able to see, touch, or feel your purpose and passion. Only your heart-touching performance can reveal to them your purposefulness. After all, the world should sense the difference between the performance of a fame-seeking, ego-centric, self-serving professional versus someone who is driven by the obsession to express his/her passion in pursuit of a higher purpose, which is not to elevate him but to elevate his Creator.

If you don't deliver unprecedented performance by outperforming everyone else in your field of passion, what does it mean? It means your purpose has not yet really touched your heart. Your passion is not fully unleashed yet.

Let your power-performance reveal to the world the power of your purpose.

Let your passion demonstrate to the world the power of passion.

Let your scorecard compel people to realize the power of your purpose and passion.

The scorecard is the best measure to see whether or not you are living your purpose and passion. If the scorecard is not impressed with your performance, that means you have not devoted everything that you have inside to your compass and heart.

Your compass and heart align together, your performance will be incomparable, unparalleled, and superlative. The lethal combination of your purpose and passion builds the momentum to put the applauding numbers on the scoreboard that no one else can match.

ALIGNING COMPASS, HEART, AND SCOREBOARD

Don't lower your expectations to meet your performance. Raise your level of performance to meet your expectations. Expect the best of yourself, and then do what is necessary to make it a reality.
- Ralph Marston

Do you want to be known as a superstar or top performer in your field? Do you wish to earn success for all the wrong motives?

Isn't it true that we all want to achieve success for all those selfish reasons i.e., money, fame, power, status, influence, etc.? That's exactly what the society pitches to each one of us.

The appeal is so tantalizing that we instantly decide to give up on our passions, divorce our purpose, and jump into the game of life without any sense of direction. We say goodbye to our own distinctive identity and decide to be someone else. We choose the wrong role models and wrong methods to chase the stuff.

We keep changing tracks, hoping to be attracted or touched by some opportunity. We wait for some magical career move that will change our life forever and realize all our dreams of having those fancy cars, penthouses, private jets, and luxury lifestyles.

Frankly, most of us don't get there. Those who get there pay a heavy price and do irreversible damage to their own self, their loved ones, and society. The most disturbing fact is that when they achieve all of that, they don't want to live that way anymore.

Performance without mission is short-lived. If performance is not backed up by passion and purpose, it will turn boring and dull.

Imagine someone steals your cell phone and enjoys the first few hours with it. Then the battery goes down, and it requires recharging. But the charger is with you. The phone is unable to perform. Soon the person discovers that only you can charge the phone. Since the phone is useless, unable to perform so the person will lose interest in it.

Similarly, when you try to follow someone's path or lifestyle, you may enjoy it for a while. But since it is not aligned with your purpose and passion, you soon lose interest.

Don't indulge in a mistaken hunt for fame and fortune. If disconnected from passion and purpose, your performance will not match with your values and principles. You will notice that your initial enthusiasm and energy is misplaced.

You may also feel that you are no more able to perform at the level you once were. You know why because you go off the path of your purpose and passion.

Stop hunting a white lie. You will never be able to convince a falsehood. Beware, upon achieving what you struggled for the whole life to achieve, instead of celebrating the joy, you may be saddened in a state of deep pain.

You don't have to respond to the false alarms around you. Supply your performance the missing passion and purpose, and you will become a force for good in the world.

If you are a purpose-driven, genuinely passionate performer, I congratulate you on producing the scoreboard's encouraging results. You are a real role model for others for delivering outstanding performance streaming from your compass and heart.

You deserve to embrace fame, money, and luxuries of life because you have attracted them through your purpose and passion. Welcome to the world of achievement and fulfillment.

An ounce of performance is worth pounds of promises.- Mae West

07 INGREDIENTS of PEAK PERFORMANCE

Whether you are in business, academia, politics, philanthropy, entertainment, media, or sports, without the following 07 components, peak performance will remain a dream. These elements will allow you to unleash your performance potential and deliver outstanding results – consistently.

1. **Goal**
   Clarity on what you want to accomplish is critical. You must have a clear vision of your performance in your mind.

2. **Preparation**
   If you skip the groundwork, everyone will eventually know that. Adequate preparation will allow you to be at your very best. You first create victory in your mind even before you take the first step. What you imagine and visualize with heartiness becomes real.

3. **Confidence**
   Your self-confidence is the ultimate armament. If you lose confidence, all-time invested in preparations will go down the drain. An unwavering belief in yourself and your purpose will lift your confidence.

4. **Drive**
   The drive is the inner life force that empowers you to face the challenges that others normally run away from. Your drive

determines your motivation level and gives you the energy to pursue your goals with focus and engagement.

5. **Intensity**
   At times the difference between two equally talented and gifted players in athletic competition is the intensity. Whether it is business or sports, your intensity will always pay off. The intensity keeps your passion alive despite setbacks, failures, and obstacles.

6. **Focus**
   The focus gives you the edge of pure concentration and the ability to handle disruptions. The focus allows you to master your emotions and get the most from each feeling you experience.

7. **Mental Toughness**
   To win the game of life, you have to be mentally tough. Mental toughness helps you build unshakeable self-belief, concentration, and single-mindedness.

   Mental and emotional toughness permits you to have meaningful and positive self-talk that builds the fortitude and spiritual connection required to beat the circumstances and secure victory.

Tick Tick Dollar is a wake-up call to connect your compass (purpose) and your heart (passion) with your scoreboard (performance)!

It is never too late to deliver your best performance.

Accept the challenges so that you can feel the exhilaration of victory.
- George S. Patton

SUMMARY
TICK TICK DOLLAR PHILOSOPHY

The complete Tick Tick Dollar™ philosophy is explained in a nutshell below:

> - First tick is a reminder for you to *live on purpose*
> - Second tick prompts you to *live your passion*
> - Dollar challenges you to *outperform* opposition in pursuit of your purpose and passion.

Begin your quest to discover your purpose and passion today. Whichever you find first, make sure that you make both aligned when you find the second one. If you find your purpose first, find the most passionate way to pursue it.

If you find your passion first, catch a way to use it to serve others, praise the Creator, and automatically find your purpose.

Remember, living every day with purpose and passion for optimum performance guarantees achievement and fulfillment.

Only a 100% commitment to maximizing your purpose, passion, and performance certifies success and prosperity. Starting from today,

'Living your purpose and passion for optimum performance' must become the slogan of your life.

Are you ready to commit to living every day outperforming competing forces in pursuit of your purpose and passion?

Tick Tick Dollar is a wake-up call to connect your compass (purpose) and your heart (passion) with your scoreboard (performance)!

It is never too late to deliver your best performance.

STAGE #1

Model	Concept
Tick	Purpose
Tick	Passion
Dollar	Performance

STAGE #2

Model	Concept	Metaphor
Tick	Purpose	Compass
Tick	Passion	Heart
Dollar	Performance	Scoreboard

STAGE #3

Model	Concept	Metaphor	Definition
Tick	Purpose	Compass	Selflessly pursuing a direction to serve people & the Creator.
Tick	Passion	Heart	Expressing your talents with love, free-will, energy, engagement, and joy.
Dollar	Performance	Scoreboard	Producing world-class results, being your best version, exceeding expectations, going the extra-mile and surprising everyone with your performance

The partnership of your compass and heart to put a massive socre on your life's scoreboard is the key to success.

Qaiser Abbas

KEY INSIGHTS:

Create a service or product that is grounded in your deepest passion. And then find the best way to *give* it to the world.

1. Purpose is giving centricity.
2. Being purpose oriented means living in a way that you serve others regardless of what you do.
3. Purpose based living is the highest form of living.
4. Giving is the most fulfilling act.
5. Passion without direction is a pain.
6. Are you giving your very best to the world? The best thing you can give to the world is the product of your passion.
7. Give your best (passion) to the world in a way that creates unprecedented success.
8. You may be giving oriented and continue to give whatever you have to the world standing outside your house. Distributing all that you have. You are a sincere giver. However, if you are unaware of a big treasure buried inside your house, you will not be able to share it with the world. Your passion is that treasure. If you don't discover it, and don't share it with the world. Your giving centricity alone will not make much difference.
9. If you know your treasure, but have not the giving mindset, the treasure will remain unutilized. It will bury with you. The only way to expand and enjoy the treasure of life is to share them with the world.
10. Don't let your passion die inside you.
11. Give life to your passion. Your passion will give lasting life to you.
12. People don't die for their passion, but for purpose, they surely do.
13. Passion is what of life, and purpose is why if life.

14. What you give to the world should be so powerful and useful that the world values it even long after you are gone.
15. There can be 100 other purposeful people, delivering the same passion to the world. However, your way of giving should inspire the world. Your delivery (performance) should be the best. Your scoreboard should be the best advertisement of your purpose and passion.
16. Ture art of living is in passion-based giving.

THINK & REFLECT

LIFE

PRINCIPLE 01

THINK & REFLECT

> Thinking is the most laborious work there is,
> which is probably why so few engage in it.
> Henry Ford

Are you where you really want to be in your life?

We all aspire to enrich our lives with a new sense of joy, pleasure, and satisfaction, but we rarely know where to start.

Most of us never seem to find the time to re-examine their lives, reorganize things, head in a new direction, and then move forward. This is like the proverbial *hard-working* woodcutter who was so *busy* chopping wood with a dull ax that he never found time to sharpen it.

Taking time out to think and reflect allows you to take a break, analyze your present situation, redefine your future priorities, and make a firm commitment to re-invigorate your life. To do this, you will have to make a few fundamental changes in your thinking and behavior. And if that induces feelings of anxiety and fear, don't worry, it's perfectly normal.

As you embark on this fantastic journey, you begin to experience a heightened sense of alertness and attentiveness to your life. If you stay committed to producing changes in your life, the reward you get will exceed your expectations.

THE MYTH OF BALANCE

Without deep reflection, one knows from daily
life that one exists for other people.
Albert Einstein

Have you ever seen a table with an uneven leg? How does it look? Lopsided. I guess all of us have had the experience of using such a table at least once in our lives.

Maybe it was a table at a roadside restaurant. You tried to place your teacup or soda pop bottle on it, but it really didn't work out. The table was continually shaking, tilting, or going over. I remember once when it happened to me; they had to place a brick under the leg to support the table. The table was trying to *perform* the job, but obviously, it was tough.

Let's look at another scenario: Imagine you are trying to change a light bulb placed high on the wall or fix something near the ceiling, and to do that, you have to stand on the same table. It's a real challenge because the uneven table can't support you. Due to its unequal legs, the entire balance is off. You are at risk of falling, right?

My friend, your life is like a table. The four table legs represent the various supports of your life. These sections should be balanced. If one leg is too long, too short, or too fragile, your life will not get enough backing.

If I push you hard to name those four vital props of your life, what would they be? Health, family, financial, intellectual, social, professional, and spiritual? If I were to choose the most essential props of your life table, they would be family, work, finance, and health.

You may not be able to spend equal amounts of time on all four areas, but you would not want anyone of those legs getting weak, shaky, or unreliable in the long run. Neglecting any one of these areas would eventually sabotage your success.

Your life can't be enriched by merely having the right work-family balance. The quality of your life will skyrocket when you involve God in all your endeavors. Once you start feeling a spiritual link with a superior power (the Almighty), life opens up new vistas, new dimensions, new opportunities, and new possibilities that you have never perceived before.

THE SEVEN THINKING VIRUSES

'The real man smiles in trouble, gathers strength from distress, and grows brave by reflection.'
Thomas Paine

Part of this reflection process would be to examine what stops you from becoming all that you can possibly be? What are the hurdles, obstacles, blockages, and barriers to your growth? Despite good intentions, most of us don't succeed because we get stuck in unproductive thinking and behavioral patterns. I call them *'viruses'.*

If unattended, these viruses can hugely damage your ability to maximize your potential, performance, and productivity. Below is a list of viruses that muddle your capability to give and be your 100%.

Our team has identified seven most toxic viruses based on our research with thousands of managers, leaders, and other professionals. Read the symptoms for each virus below carefully and candidly reflect which viruses have already infected your thoughts and behavior. The next step would be to devise some strategies to protect you against them.

1. 'I hate goals'

This virus signifies a mindset that encourages having no goals at all. I would remind you of the metaphor of playing football without goalposts, which results only in exhaustion. Without clear goals in life, people suffer from the same feeling of tiredness.

Some people even deceive themselves into believing that they have goals, but their goals are either non-existent or completely blurred.

This virus is not very difficult to cure. You just need to sit down with a pen and a few sheets of paper and write down your goals. We will learn the art of goal setting in the next chapter.

2. 'I love mess'

People suffering from this syndrome are in love with the mess. They have this tendency to appreciate mess, create a mess, accumulate mess, multiply mess, and live with the mess. Their desk, drawers, cabinet, filing system, and everything else will present a mess and chaos.

They also have this infectious ability to spread this mess to others. These people are best described as '*disorganized*'. This virus nullifies your ability to think clearly.

Your untidy workstation and cluttered environment make it almost impossible for you to find documents, papers, or files that an important client or your boss may urgently require. Since your workstation is jumbled and chaotic, you find it almost impossible to *retrieve* things and information from your computer, drawers, cabinets, etc. You can't even find phone numbers when you need them the most.

Studies have also proved that working with a messy desk wastes an hour and a half per day looking for things or being distracted by things. That's seven and a half hours per week.

3. **'I enjoy living with the crisis.'**

"When a deadline sneaks up on me, it robs me of all choice, and I am controlled by the clock" is a common gripe for crisis-mania victims. Crisis brings lots of stress, pressure, and worry with it. How would you know if you have this virus in your system? One symptom is letting things slip through the cracks and often having to go back and redo what was not done correctly in the first place.

The virus is undoubtedly widespread if you leave important things to the last minute. When you don't act at the appropriate time, you invite a crisis to inflict havoc on your life. The truth is that when you complain to others, 85% of them really don't care, and the other 15% are secretly delighted deep inside that it's happening to you.

However, there is good news for you. 90% of all those crises are preventable. A crisis can be pre-empted by ensuring action at the right time.

4. **'I find it difficult to say no'**

'Would you please help me with my quarterly sales review report?' a fellow manager pleads.

Now you know this is not your job, you are already overloaded with your own work, you don't have the time, you don't have the expertise and resources, and you don't even want to do it, BUT your response to the request is *'yes, sure... ....'*

But when you had so many reasons to say NO, how could you even consider saying YES? When I ask my participants the same question in workshops, their answers go something like:

1. *I didn't want to refuse. I didn't want them to think I am incompetent.*
2. *They would have thought I was discourteous.*
3. *Why would I let them think I am incapable of multi-tasking?*
4. *I was fearful of damaging my reputation.*

What happens if you start saying *'yes, sure'* to every unreasonable request? You risk unfavorable attacks and undesirable results. You probably over-commit yourself, miss out on essential tasks, and your level of work pressure increases, you feel anxious, worried, and stressed.

Before you say yes to anything, ask yourself, *"Is this the best use of my time?"* If it is, do it. If not, think about saying NO more often.

5. 'I adore interruptions'

You can easily spot people in your office who *invite* people to interrupt them. They love disturbances, especially if they are a total wastage of time. They are *prone* to all types of interruptions. Their slogan is *'Please disturb'*. If they don't find someone to disturb them, they will embark on a round of the office to discover people they can disturb.

And if they are unsuccessful at that, they somehow manage to create the same impact through technological gadgets like phones and emails, etc. Since they are committed to time-wasting devices, they make confident that they have an adequate supply of human and technological interruptions to fill their quota.

Interruption lovers also have the tendency to get infected by another virus called *'meetingitis'*. This virus is characterized by spending too much time in utterly unproductive meetings. So what is the cure? Very simple: before committing to a meeting, ask, *'Is it really indispensable?'*

6. 'I hate planning'

If you are a planning hater, the only place for plans in your life is a garbage *'bin. '* You think of your memory as an unbeatable storage area and therefore perceive no need to plan or write anything out in the form of a project. You think writing is a waste of time.

Whatever is in your mind, put it on paper. Don't put your plans in the bin; put them in your ideas journal instead. When you write it down and look at it, there is less chance of forgetting something. Keep that golden principle in mind *'Out of sight, out of mind'*, and the opposite of that is correct too: *'In sight, in mind'*.

7. 'I am happy to be lazy'

Why would anyone put off doing something of prime importance when doing it at the right time would result in reward, and not doing it doesn't offer any benefit? Laziness discourages people from doing things; they tend to postpone things.

I regard putting off *unimportant* things as a handy talent. Unfortunately, the Laziness virus *inspires* us to procrastinate about the important ones.

Remember Southwest Airline's annual strategic plan that uses the promotional slogan '*doing things*'? However, this virus doesn't allow us to move forward, take action, and achieve success.

All the planning in the world is no proxy for actually doing something. So stop being a lazy-crazy person and start accomplishing your goals like a winner.

ACTIONS

We cannot solve our problems with the same
thinking we used when we created them.
Albert Einstein

1. Know where you are?
2. What is working and what is not working
3. Identify which 'viruses' are blocking your way to a more fabulous life?

"Many people seem to think that success in one area can compensate for failure in other areas. But can it really? True effectiveness requires balance."
-- Stephen Covey

IGNITE FUTURE

IGNITE FUTURE

'Eyes are to dream'

'You can't connect the dots looking forward; you can only connect them looking backwards. So you have to trust that the dots will somehow connect in your future. You have to trust in something - your gut, destiny, life, karma, whatever. This approach has never let me down, and it has made all the difference in my life'. Steve Jobs

Is it possible to see the future right now? For most of us, this requires unique talents and know-how of magic. However, every successful person knows that it doesn't require any unusual flairs or gifts.

Every human has been conferred with the knack of seeing the future finished in advance. All that requires is to close your eyes and begin to see what you want to see in the future. This chapter is filled with tools and processes to help you *'ignite'* your future.

Put your current limitations, hurdles, obstacles, and roadblocks aside. Imagine you got a magic wand that can make all of your dreams and wishes come alive. What would you like to wave this magic wand for?

> *"My interest is in the future because I am going to spend the rest of my life there."* Charles Kettering

The best way to ignite your future is to ask yourself this 100 million dollar question:

"If you are given a guarantee of success, an assurance that you can never fail in anything; what would you like to do"?

- What would you like to be?
- What would you like to try?
- What risks would you like to take?
- What ventures will you like to become part of?
- What adventures would you like to go?
- What fears would you like to face?
- What limits would you like to break?
- What challenges would you like to accept?
- What dangers would you like to embrace?
- What problems would you like to solve?
- What experiments would you like to perform?
- What hypothesis would you like to test?
- What assumptions would you like to validate?
- What decisions would you like to make?
- What initiatives would you like to pursue?
- What moves would you like to make?
- What leaps would you like to take?

Are these questions good enough to ignite your future? Have you already taken off to a day-dream flight?

> 'A dream is your creative vision for your life in the future. You must break out of your current comfort zone and become comfortable with the unfamiliar and the unknown.' Denis Waitley

Igniting your future will allow you to see, explore, and design the bigger picture. Life is like a jigsaw puzzle. If you know the picture in advance, it becomes much easier to put all pieces in the right place. It saves time and effort. Not knowing the picture leaves you with the only option to hit and trial method. At times, it gets so frustrating and disappointing that we leave the puzzle in the middle and give up.

So if you know you can't fail and have no constraints, why would you not go for accomplishing more? Why would you limit yourself to do only a few things? Would your endeavors focus only on your gains, or would you benefit the whole society from this unique opportunity?

When I did the same exercise the first time, I was on the street having no place to live. Yet, I came up with a list of 764 dreams, hopes, and ambitions. Today, if I look back, I have achieved most of them. That is an indicator that I was not dreaming too big.

YOUR BIG PICTURE

'If you don't dream, you are virtually blind.'

> 'Yesterday is but today's memory, and tomorrow is today's dream'. Khalil Gibran

I cannot over-emphasize the importance of having a bigger picture of your life. By the big picture, I mean your overall vision about your life, what purpose drives that vision, what personal identity you require to support your vision and purpose, and what short-term and long-term goals you should set to reach (*or exceed as I did*) your vision of life.

What do you really want to do with your life? What do you want to create? If you possessed the same energy you had as a child, what would you like to accomplish? What is it that would get you out of bed early and keep you up late at night?

When you ponder these questions, dynamic and exciting ideas begin to stream into your mind. You set in motion the process of determining what your life vision is.

Without a clear understanding of what your life would be like, say about ten years from now, any attempt to change the way you live today will be wasted. So push yourself hard to get your correct inner answers to the questions I asked above.

SEEING THE INVISIBLE

'If you think in terms of a year, plant a seed; if in terms of ten years, plant trees; if in terms of 100 years, teach the people.' - Confucius

What does your vision of life look like? If you had no fear of moving forward, what would you do with your life? What hurdles might you be motivated to overcome? What contributions would you like to make to your own life and the lives of others? If you knew you could have it any way you want, what would you want out of your life? What do you want to be, to give, create, feel, or share?

Did you feel any sense of excitement when you were reading these questions? Probably they made you feel uncomfortable rather than excited. Why, because a part of you wanted to work on these questions and the other part sensed that answering them would be stressful.

That other part of you was fearful of digging deeper into your inner awareness. So you weren't motivated enough to do it, and you *skipped* answering these questions. Don't let this negative part of you win the battle. Go back; reread them and figure out your answers.

THE SENSE OF MISSION

> *'The future belongs to those who believe in the beauty of their dreams.'* Eleanor Roosevelt

Why must you achieve this vision? What is the ultimate purpose of your life? How will it benefit you to achieve this vision in your life? How will that make you feel? Ultimately, why do you want to achieve that vision? Whose lives will you touch in the process?

What is the purpose that would drive you to eliminate the obstacles that hold you back? How would it feel to achieve the vision for your life? What emotions do you want to experience as a result?

The idea of having a vision and purpose for your life is not something I invented. It is not an original idea of mine, unlike many other ideas I am presenting in this book. I discovered these *vision provoking* thoughts in some personal development books many years ago, but I never gave serious consideration to them. The result? I remained where I was: In my mentor, Jim Rohn's words, *'pennies in the pocket, nothing in the bank, creditors calling.'*

'Hold fast to dreams, for if dreams die, life is a broken-winged bird that cannot fly.' Langston Hughes

The day I was inspired to discover my real purpose and vision, my goals automatically flowed. After following the process, I created an unbelievable alignment between my purpose, vision, values, and goals. That day I wrote out some 764 dreams I yearned to achieve. Surprisingly, I started achieving them – and that too at a much faster pace than I could imagine.

Please go back to the vision and mission section (if you skipped it) and spend some quality time answering them. They will reveal new answers that will make significant contributions to your success, happiness, and prosperity.

IDENTITY

'All men dream, but not equally. Those who dream by night in the dusty recesses of their minds wake in the day to find that it was vanity: but the dreamers of the day are dangerous men, for they may act on their dreams with open eyes, to make them possible.' T. E. Lawrence

Your self-discovery journey will be unfinished if you don't find out your real identity. Have you given a series of thought to the question, "Who are you?" How do you define yourself?

What metaphors do you use to describe yourself? What object would you like to borrow from the universe to explain who you are? A candle? A mountain? A river? A sword? A map? A volcano? A train engine? A music instrument? A flower?

What is the essence of who you are? What roles do you play? If you were to look up your name in a dictionary, what would it say? What are some of the characteristics you exemplify (or aspire to exemplify)?

What is it that you stand for in your life? Forget your past – who and what kind of person are you now? What have you decided to become? What are the standards you have set for your life - physically, emotionally, spiritually, financially, and socially?

This exercise gives you food for thought about the way you perceive yourself. With this enhanced awareness of your vision, purpose, and identity, what do you want to feel or experience in your life?

To me, success is turning nothing into something. To build your great future tomorrow, you must ignite the future in your mind today. What you will see today will become a resounding reality tomorrow. You cannot predict the future, so you better put your heart and soul to create it. Start igniting the future today!

COMMIT 100%

COMMIT 100%

> *"The quality of a person's life is in direct proportion to their commitment to excellence, regardless of their chosen field of endeavor."* - Vince Lombardi

Commitment matters. To step up to the next level, commitment matters. Commitment means keeping your words. Taking the leap. Trying when giving up is easy. Embracing discomfort. Running to your fears. Daring to stand out from the crowd. Commitment means leading your life, not just living it, and be the best you.

Living your dreams is never the result of an accident. Nothing changes overnight. Success meets only those who show resolve and courage to invest in pursuing their dream life. They devote their heart, mind, and soul in line with their purpose. Committed people use their time, intelligence, and resources with laser focus to move toward their desired future.

It doesn't matter which profession you are in; if you commit to excellence, you will stand out from the crowd. Success eludes those who remain shaky when it is time to demonstrate dedication. Commitment is the live demonstration of purpose and passion in action. Nothing has ever been achieved by any human being without commitment.

WHAT IS COMMITMENT?

'Success depends upon previous preparation, and without such preparation, there is sure to be a failure.'
Confucius

Commitment is a pledge to keep going regardless of whatever comes in the way. It's an assurance of effort, struggles, determination. Making a commitment means you will never give up. It's a promise to continue your search for a better tomorrow. Commitment is a declaration of not leaving a goal in the middle. Committing 100% means guaranteeing to apply all your force, energy, and sweat to do whatever it takes to make quest dreams a reality.

100% commitment turns nothing into something. 100% commitment can move mountains. 100% commitment can make a dent in the universe. 100% commitment is an oath to be your very best: to polish your skills, master the strategies, overcome your weaknesses, surmount your shortcomings, and defeat the odds.

Commitment 100% means giving your 100% and being prepared to sacrifice your time, energy, resources, money, rest, and sleep to realize your goals.

Commitment means risking everything you have and standing by to pay the price no matter what it is for achieving your vision and making a firm decision to never give up until you get what you want.

MIRACLE OF COMMITMENT

> *You see, greatness for a state doesn't require some massive monument for all to see. It is not a journey to a particular destination - but a commitment to follow a course of constant and never-ending improvement.* - Sonny Perdue

Commitment breeds ownership. When you are committed to a relationship, you begin to own that person. You feel for the person. You do your best to make that person feel protected, loved, cared, and comforted. You take a stand for the person. Similarly, when you commit to achieving a goal, you exhibit the highest devotion and resolve.

Commitment ignites a renewed sense of responsibility. When fully committed, people take full responsibility for making their dream real. The blames and complaints run away automatically. There is no room for excuses in your life.

Remember when you were fully committed to attending the wedding ceremony of a friend in a remote city. You overcame all the constraints of money, resources, and time because you were ready to think creatively. You found innovative solutions to every problem that raised on the day.

When in a commitment frame of mind, people focus on finding a solution rather than sticking to the problems. Solution-mindedness opens the doors of new opportunities to you. When committed, people never accept 'No' as an answer. They always find their way.

TEST OF COMMITMENT

If you schedule it, you commit to doing it.

> *You cannot escape the responsibility of tomorrow by evading it today.* - Abraham Lincoln

To me, the only test of commitment it time. What does that mean?

If I am really committed to something, I will take time out to work on it. Whether it is a relationship or a goal, if you are fully committed to it, you will always find the time.

Person A: *I am committed to staying fit and healthy*
Person B: *What was the last time you found yourself in the gym or park for exercise?*
Person A: *I can't remember exactly, but it was some three months before!*

You can see the level of commitment here?

If you are genuinely committed to doing something, you will indeed find time in your schedule to get it done. Conversely, if a goal fails to find some space in your daily schedule, you are obviously not fully committed.

What you are genuinely committed to reflecting in your goals, priorities, and, most importantly, daily schedules.

> *You need to make a commitment, and once you make it, life will give you some answers.* - Les Brown

Who doesn't want to be a winner? To win, you need to stick to a plan. That requires commitment—daily intensity. Your commitment is reflected in your daily living. When not fully committed, you respond to the most vociferous voices around. You sacrifice your own priorities. Committing 100% is not doing the wrong things faster. It is doing the right thing only.

What is the opposite of commitment? Compromise! When we compromise, we settle on less than the best. We give up on our dreams. We end up selling our dreams and exchange them with pains, dissatisfaction, and emptiness. By compromising on less than the best, we stop us from becoming all we are meant to be. We withhold the gifts given to us by our creator. We live a life of mediocrity, guilt, and shame.

> *Desire is the key to motivation, but it's determined and committed to an unrelenting pursuit of your goal - a commitment to excellence - that will enable you to attain the success you seek.*
> Mario Andretti

RULES OF (staying out of) THE GAME:

Despite having clearly defined destination and resources, most of the people remain where they are. You know why? Two reasons:

1. They don't know what is stopping them
2. They don't know the rules of the game

Based on my years of study of why people don't act now and waste years in inaction, I have devised nine rules.

Understanding the rules will allow you to adjust your game and apply your talent to get the desired results.

1. BEING EAGER IS NOT ENOUGH

Most of us are very eager to kick start positive changes in our lives. We are enthusiastic about implementing a new diet plan, join the new sports, reading the latest book we bought, exercising in the new health club that we took membership for, playing with our kids, or attending the upcoming training seminar.

However, we all have witnessed our eagerness fading in a couple of days. We forget where the gardening gadgets are, we forget to follow through on our exercise, reading, skill development, parenting responsibilities.

We are genuinely enthused to kickoff new activity, plan, or project. Yet, our keenness dwindles in the next few days. And if we knew in advance as a rule of thumb that our eagerness alone is not enough, we would not have relied on it in the first place. Remember, being eager is not bad. Indeed it is a great start. However, advanced knowledge of its fickleness would allow you to have some backup plans too.

2. WILL POWER WILL ONLY TAKE YOU THAT FAR

Like enthusiasm, willpower is a great beginning. It can give you the initial energy boost, but to kick start a new idea or a project successfully, you need much more than that. There will be times when your will power will fade.

The environment around us is filled with distractions and attractions that can unfavorably affect our willpower and self-control. Therefore, you need to instill some mechanisms and external controls also to completely follow through on something you kickoff.

3. KNOWLEDGE IS NOT ENOUGH

If you know something, there is no guarantee you will be doing something about it too. Knowing and doing are two different worlds. Remember, knowledge alone will take you nowhere.

What we know is very impressive. But what we do is quite shocking. I believe your actions should speak louder than your knowledge. I urge you to live life so that you are re-remembered by your action, not by your knowledge.

4. SIMPLE IS FORGETTABLE

Have you seen yourself taking a job too easy and then forgetting to do a crucial part of that simple task? Why did you forget that? Because you thought it is so easy and straightforward, and why should I forget that? Yet, you overlooked some critical elements of that simple task that cost you either re-work or loads of mental stress.

The human brain needs some structure to carry out even the simplest tasks. At times we are caught in the simplicity trap and fail to provide ourselves an essential foundation to take the right action at the right time in the right manner.

Don't take any change too easy to implement, or too simple to execute. Give yourself a step-by-step process, structure, or a checklist to ensure smooth action. From cleaning a bathroom to flying an airplane, an essential checklist will help you a long way to remember all the critical elements and do a great job.

5. EXPECT THE UNEXPECTED

How many times you initiate a project with enthusiasm. You were regular. And then something happens. Now it's been over two weeks since you have not been to the gym. Why did you discontinue?

Because something unexpected happened, and your plan had no room for that. Without expecting the unexpected, no plan is complete.

6. YOU ARE SPECIAL, NOT THE DAY

Remember the time when you had recently started going to the gym? You were regular, punctual, and disciplined. You were enjoying the process and gaining the right results. And suddenly you stopped going to the gym. You failed to follow through on your initial commitment to regular exercise and staying in shape.

If you look back and reflect on what caused you to interrupt your regular pattern. The answer will be what you considered a 'special' day.

What is a special day? A day when you decided to skip the process telling yourself that I don't need to act on my routine (i.e., going to the gym) because today is an exception. Examples of a special day would include:

1. It is my birthday
2. It's a Sunday or a weekend
3. Today is Eid
4. This is Christmas
5. It is our National Day or Independence Day.
6. I have invited friends for dinner
7. It's very hot or freezing
8. It's raining today
9. It's my daughter's first day at school
10. I am tired
11. It's my wedding day or a family wedding or friend's wedding

We give ourselves a concession for all these special days so that we take a break from whatever is necessary.

7. NO CHANGE IS PERMANENT

Most of us become victims of this trap. We produce change. We enjoy the reward. Then we go to sleep. Expecting the change will last forever. On its own. Wrong!

If you exercise regularly, build the right body and think the story ends here. You are wrong. You must know that no change is permanent. Unless you work to make it permanent. If you didn't pay attention to this rule, you would end up reproducing the same change.

8. PROBLEM FREE LIFE IS A MYTH

The happy ending exists in movies and fairy tales only. Our wrong thinking convinces us that if the current problem is solved. It will never reoccur. This can be true. But what is the assurance that a *new* problem will not arise?

Like it or not, you will never live a problem-free life. Good news: you can learn to rise above problems. You can build strength to turn problems into blessings—hurdles into opportunities. And build more critical skills to handle them.

9. YOU ARE NOT THE BEST JUDGE

Psychology has proved it over and over again that we overestimate our abilities and talents. We underestimate others' abilities and talents.

Therefore, you should not be judging your own growth. You have a tendency to give your favorable ratings. You are biased.

You think you are best when in reality, you are not. Face the reality today. See yourself from a neutral eye and spot the gaps. Take a step to fill those gaps and begin your quest today toward your goals.

BUILDING YOUR LIFE

An elderly contractor was ready to retire. He told his employer of his plans to leave the house-building business to live a more comfortable life.

The employer reluctantly agreed; however, he asked the contractor to build just one last house as a personal favor.

The contractor didn't want to say yes, but the employer was overly insistent. So he hesitantly agreed. But he was not 100% committed. He was obviously a little revengeful too.

Over time it was easy to see that his heart was not in his work. He didn't bother much about the design of the house. He resorted to shoddy workmanship and used inferior materials.

He knew all the fundamental principles of building a great house, but he didn't fully practice them here. In a hurry, he didn't even give this house a finishing touch. It was an unfortunate way to end a dedicated career.

When the contractor finished his work, his employer came to inspect the house. Then he handed the front-door key to the contractor and said:

"This is your house... my gift to you."

The carpenter was shocked!

Deep inside in heart, he was regretfully telling himself, *"What a shame! If I had only known I was building my own house, I would have done it all so differently."*

As the contractor, we all are contractors of our own life. We build our lives, one day at a time, often putting less than our best into the building. Not committing 100%. Then, with a shock, we realize we have to live in the house we have built. If we could do it over, we would do it much differently.

Can you commit to applying all the principles you already know to build your great life?

KICKOFF NOW

PRINCIPLE 04

KICKOFF NOW

> *"When I started the race, the only thing I could see was the finish line."*
>
> Naseem Hameed
> The Fastest Woman in South Asia, 11th South Asian Games
> Great daughter of Pakistan

'I know what to do. I recognize the benefits of doing it. I understand the negative consequences of not doing it. I have the competence and resources to do it. But I still don't do it.'

Does this story sound familiar?

Why would you delay heading in the direction of your dreams?

Why would you not kickoff now?

What is stopping you from staying away from your higher life?

What benefits will you reap by delaying this move?

Not kicking-off now also puts a big question mark on your commitment. If you are indeed 100% committed, why would you not take action now?

There could be three probable reasons:

1. There is no sense of urgency
2. You are stuck in the comfort trap
3. You are held by your self-doubt

I am sure you will agree that you often encounter reasons not letting you kickoff. You prefer postponing the next steps. You give in to the causes keeping you from doing what is critical for your own success. You don't have to give in to these energy-sucking reasons and become victims of procrastination. If you didn't take charge, you would be left with a big list of incompletes in all significant areas of your life.

Why would you leave yourself at the mercy of '*The Guilt of the Incompletes*'?

7 DREADFUL BEHAVIORS

"Well begun is half done."
— *Aristotle*

Our research reveals the following behaviors, not allowing people to kickoff now when they should have taken immediate action.

1. Waiting for the right mood:
   You don't feel like doing it. Your mood is off, and you are emotionally down.

2. Waiting for the right time:

You don't think that this is the right time to take action when actually it is.

3. Lack of clear goals:
    You started but did not have a clear idea about what was expected. You did not know the performance criteria. You finally got around to doing it, but the task was too vague, unclear, and blurred.

    As a result, you did not find a good reason to continue. How can you feel inclined to do it when the goal is not clear?

4. Underestimating the difficulty:
    You thought doing it was no big deal, but when you started, you realized that you would have to put in much more effort than you first thought. So why not postpone it for now?

5. Underestimating the time required:
    Your initial judgment of the time necessary to reach the finish line of your goal is wrong. Upon knowing it is going to take much more time than you thought dulls your motivation to even start. Therefore, delaying it is the smoothest call.

6. Feeling the goal is imposed on you:
    When you think you *have* to do it, your enthusiasm is reduced. Your heart and mind are not fully involved.

7. Perfectionism:
    '*I don't have the right skills or resources to do this perfectly, so I won't do it.*'

Did you find that some of these reasons played a significant role in diminishing your life quality? Did you also find yourself using some of these causes to hold you back?

FEAR IS THE REAL ENEMY OF ACTION

Regardless of the number of books they read or training sessions they attend, some people do not demonstrate even an iota of improvement in their results. Why? After acquiring all the tools, techniques, and strategies, why do people not put what they know into practice? Why do people choose inaction instead of taking action?

We have identified some psychological fears. I call them blockages to human performance and productivity. You are not consciously aware of these fears.

You will probably never admit that these fears are there, buried deep in your heart. But a psychological analysis conducted professionally will reveal that underlying your lack of achievement is a range of fears that do not allow your inner creativity and potential free rein.

These fears suppress your inventiveness; your talents and resources remain hidden, undeveloped, and untapped. These fears include:

1. What if I fail?
    If I were unsuccessful, how would I handle the embarrassment? It's better not to show up for this presentation. Let's delay it.

2. What if I succeed?
    If I did it this time, people would expect me to do it again. Will I be able to handle the pressure that comes with success?

3. What if I get hurt?
    If the status quo is disturbed, who knows how the new situation will turn out? Let's maintain things as they are. Why take a risk?

4. What if I am wrong?

If I started it now, I would not leave it until it is done at the right level. Do I have time to take it to that level?

5. What if I lose in the end?
If I did it now, I might end up losing out on a few things. Can I handle the loss?

Did you recognize any of your fears above?

ART OF BEATING DELAYS

What is the opposite of 'delay'?

To beat 'delays', you need to install antidote in your system - 'kickoff!'

Beating delays require resolving, sense of urgency, and persistence, which is the opposite of postponement. The simplest definition of procrastination is 'never *getting started*'. Moving a step ahead, this definition will also include 'not *finishing things that you started*'.

To transform deferment into persistence, let me share a powerful thought with you:

Remember your mother helping you eat that large bread by breaking it up into small pieces, so you could eat it one piece at a time? That's precisely the strategy you can utilize to defeat stalling. It doesn't matter what you are up to; planning to write a book, make your new video, prepare an important presentation, aim to make a world-class painting, design a website, or climb a mountain. The key to success is your ability to break down the task into convenient, bite-size chunks and knock them off *at a time.*

You can see the same principle in action while reading this book: one page at a time. You may not be surprised to learn that I utilized the principle while writing this book: one page, one principle, one topic at a time.

TURN ON

Some people think of themselves as born procrastinators. They can manufacture the most beautiful, sophisticated, and real-sounding *justifications* in the world.

I was a procrastinator most of my life until I discovered the art of *'turning myself on'*. How can you use the art of 'turning yourself on'? Simply think it through and anticipate all those great rewards that will come as a result of *kicking-off*.

As you think of delaying some critical move, your mind instantly presents the 'logical reasons' to support your decision. Don't waste the creative juices of your mind in inventing excuses. Consume them instead to visualize the big payoff you will get if you kickoff now.

PAYOFFS

For instance, you wish to build a professional relationship with a very high profile business person. Still, you feel an inner reluctance to take the initiative and explore the opportunities to connect. So how do you motivate yourself not to delay?

The right approach would be to visualize all the many advantages that could accrue from the relationship from the other people in their network. You can be introduced to various new contacts and the likelihood of working together on various projects.

After seeing these benefits, your mind will instantly push you to take immediate action and will reject any lame excuse to put it off.

OPEN NOTICE

After learning how to '*turn yourself on*' to overcome procrastination, get ready to '*turn others on*'. How do you do that?

It is effortless: tell a lot of people about something you wish to get done but has been delaying it. Not only you tell them what you wish to accomplish, and your deadline for doing it, but also request them to keep reminding you about it as frequently as possible.

What will happen? Every time you bump into these people, they will start *monitoring* your progress and ask about the status of your goals. Their question could be something like this:

- So did you make any progress?
- What have you done so far to reach your goal?
- Will, you once again *not* meet your deadlines?
- How long will we have to wait before you complete this long-awaited goal?
- Are you serious about the goal or just trying to impress us?

These painful reminders are indeed wake-up calls. The questions will boost your morale and stimulate your emotional energy to fight the deadly disease of postponement. After all, why would you like to be embarrassed in front of your close associates? You don't want to be labeled as a chronic procrastinator?

DELAY SYMPTOMS

How would you recognize the symptoms of delays? I am sharing some of the signs below. Hopefully, you will identify yours:

1. Filling your day with low priority activities
2. Reading an e-mail more than once without doing anything about it

3. Starting a high-priority task, and almost immediately going off to make you a coffee or check your Facebook page.
4. Leaving an item on your *to-do* list undone for a long time, even though you know it's important

ANTI DELAY TECHNIQUE

The tendency to procrastinate is a syndrome that has the potential to negatively impact your results, success, even your entire life. Taking the initiative and making things happen at the right time is the need of the day.

PAIN & PLEASURE

One psychological reason for not programming ourselves to take immediate action on a crucial assignment is that we have no real awareness of the pain involved in not doing it or the pleasure we will get from completing it.

To get yourself enthused about something you have been putting off, create a sense of the pain you will feel as a result of not doing it or how much pleasure you will get from doing it. What will be your motivation, pain, or pleasure? I daresay you opt for *pleasure*!

IMAN TECHNIQUE

I have created a strategy to defeat delays and build results faster. I call it the **IMAN** technique.

I
Must
Act
Now!

So, are you ready to *act now*?

TRACK GOALS

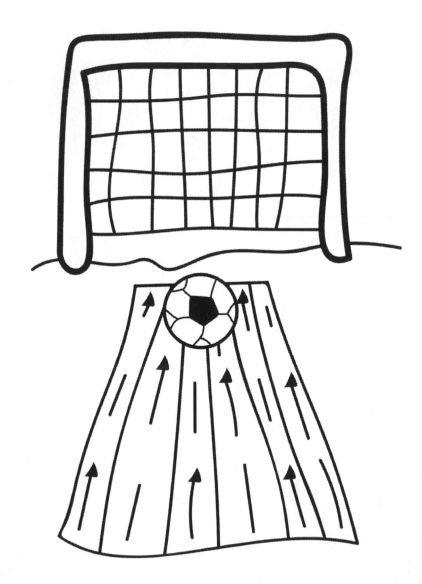

TRACK GOALS

> "If you set goals and go after them with all the determination you can muster, your gifts will take you places that will amaze you."
> Les Brown

Have you ever played football without having goalposts? During a training course, I once got the senior executives of a bank to try the experience of playing football without goalposts.

What happened? After a few minutes, they were all confused, exhausted, and drained. There was a lot of activity but zero productivity. They had no strategy, no plans, no coordination, and enthusiasm at any point in the game. Eventually, they lost interest and decided to abandon the game.

This is precisely what happens when we live a life without clear-cut goals. We end up feeling exhausted and drained but achieve no significant success. Eventually, we lose our enthusiasm to carry on and call the game of life off.

The key to success and prosperity has clear-cut, understandable, and unambiguous goals. I suggest you re-look at all the major areas of your life and set goals.

GOAL SETTING GUIDELINES

Below is a guideline for goal setting.

FINANCIAL:

There is nothing wrong about wanting more money. Money can help you attain heights that you never could accomplish without it. Set a goal to become a millionaire.

About 17 years ago, when my monthly income was a mere 18$, I decided to aim 10 times more than that. Guess what?

Now (and this is not to impress you), my training fee for a single day is approximately 1000 times more than I was making in the entire month – and the credit goes to the Tick Tick Dollar™ philosophy. How much do you want to earn by a certain age? What is holding you back?

CAREER:

To support your financial goals, you need to have clear-cut career goals. What level do you want to attain in your career? What will your career aspirations ultimately lead you to?

At what position you want to get retired? Where would you be on your career ladder ten years from now?

EDUCATION:

You will probably agree with me that elevating your career to new heights is possible with the right skillset and education. Do you need to acquire a new degree? Is there any knowledge, in particular, you need to acquire?

What expertise and skills will you need to achieve your goals? What books do you need to read? What self-development program do you need to take? Remember, what goes in comes out.

I read a beautiful thought somewhere a few years ago that deeply impacted my personal development initiatives and philosophy: 'Put better ideas in your mind, and your mind will give you better performance.'

PHYSICAL:

Don't you need excellent health and fitness to achieve your educational, financial, and career goals? What goals will help to ensure a sustained level of energy and vitality?

Are there any athletic feats you want to achieve, or do you want to enjoy good health well into the old age? What steps can you take to achieve perfect physical health and fitness?

ARTISTIC:

Do you have any unique talents or artistic abilities and want to harness them? Do you want to learn to play some musical instruments? Do you want to take art classes?

Do you wish to be the center of attention at family gatherings because of your unique talents and performing arts abilities?

ATTITUDE:

Do you get negative feedback from your close friends about your attitude? Are there any feelings, emotions, or attitudes that may become obstacles to your future growth?

Is any part of your mindset holding you back? Is there any part of the way you behave upsets you and others? If so, set a goal to improve your behavior or find a solution to the problem.

PLEASURE:

What gives you pleasure? What experiences would you like to go through? Do you aim to embark on such extreme sports experiences as paragliding, canoeing, sky diving, rock climbing, skiing, parachuting, etc.?

What other activities do you have in mind that can give you a feeling of joy, pleasure, thrill, and excitement?

FAMILY:

What are your aspirations for your family? What quality of life would you wish to provide for your family? What experiences would you wish to share with your family?

Do you wish to be a parent? If so, how are you going to be a good parent? How would you like to be seen by your kids? What your kids will be most proud of about you? How do you wish to be perceived by your spouse or by members of your extended family? How do you wish to create feelings of pride in your parents?

CONTRIBUTION:

How can the world become a better place because of you? What can you share, contribute, and give to this world? What goals would you set to improve the quality of life around you?

You may also find that these goals are deeply connected and interdependent. When you seriously work on them, you will notice that success in one-goal may leverage your overall success as the attainment of one goal is often interlinked.

At this stage, your task is to just figure out your aspirations in each area of your life. You don't have to worry about plans, strategies, and specifications.

The primary purpose is to write down the ideas streaming through your mind; the objective is to give free rein to your imagination and dare to think big.

The next stage is to take these ideas forward and convert them into SMART Goals.

PRICE of ACHIEVING GOALS

Price is what you pay. Value is what you get.
Warren Buffett

Over the last fourteen years, I have read so much on setting and achieving goals. I have had the privilege to work with the most successful superstars of sports, movies, and business. My job as a success coach is to help them set and achieve their goals.

These goals include producing an award-winning movie, winning the gold medal in Olympics, writing a best-selling book, winning the series against the most robust sports team, or achieving the target for business growth.

The vision of life, dreams, purpose, and goals remained unaccomplished until we learn to pay the price for achieving our most desired goals. Yes, the keyword here is PRICE.

Why am I putting so much emphasis on PRICE? The reason is that without a system that can ensure your progress in achieving goals, the journey toward success is half-finished.

So let's begin the process of using the PRICE philosophy to create an extraordinary life.

PRECISE

Goals that are not precisely defined don't get you to the finishing line. You have to be absolutely clear even about microscopic details. A well-defined, clear-cut, positively stated goal is hard to miss.

If you want to own a car, be precise about color, model, size, price, and other relevant details. Many people set goals that are not exact, detailed, accurate, and specific; this lack of clarity doesn't allow them to achieve their most cherished goals. Developing crystal-clear goals is a guarantee of achieving them.

ROUSING

No matter how specific the goal is if it doesn't motivate you, forget about it. Motivation is the fuel that keeps your goals' train moving. A rousing goal excites you, fills your heart and mind with energy, and kindles you to take action.

Take a look at your current goals and randomly pick up any one of them. Do you feel energized to view the goal? Do you think your goal is inspiring enough to excite and engage you?

For any goal to become a reality, it has to be 'rousing,' thrilling and stirring enough to stimulate your resources and capacities.

If you don't feel particularly inspired by your goal, you can add secondary motivators to excite yourself. My friend Umer Khan was employed as an area sales manager at the beginning of his career.

He didn't feel particularly enthusiastic about visiting clients, but he had to find the motivation to visit his clients, dealers in a geographically scattered territory. He kept thinking of ways to galvanize himself and finally found out that he was always enthused by eating out.

He identified various eating spots close to each customer's office. That provided him the rousing feel to visit the customers because it would also take him to his favorite dining venues.

Work out your primary motivation for achieving your goals. If you don't find any, spur your enthusiasm with secondary motivations.

IMPORTANT

You cannot move an inch toward a goal if you don't find it essential. High importance goals automatically become a priority and focus of your attention. How many goals in your list are unimportant? Do you think you will ever do anything about them?

By important, I mean that the goals have to be relevant to the overall purpose, vision, and big picture of your life.

A person aspiring to become a world swimming champion should not waste time becoming a tennis champion in college. For example, your educational goal to acquire a degree should also support the bigger picture of your career.

CHASE-ABLE

The goal should be moderately difficult. Not so fierce that no one has ever achieved it, nor so easy that it doesn't give you a feeling of accomplishment. Research carried out on successful people reveals that they set moderately tricky targets.

Chase-ability is more of a time factor. If you allow the right amount of time to chase your goals, you may one day even spend a vacation on the moon. However, if you aim to do so by next week, it will probably not be chase-able.

Setting moderately severe goals builds your confidence, enabling you to accept and achieve more challenging goals in the future.

ESTIMABLE

Without estimating the goal progress, you will be lost in the fog of your daily routine. Devise a system for keeping track of your daily improvements. Some organizations refer to it as 'daily intensity.'

If not daily, you should at least be able to measure the progress weekly or monthly. Otherwise, you will find that no progress has been made on a goal that was otherwise precise, rousing, important, and exceedingly chase-able.

Your key takeaway from this chapter should be a clear understanding of what is important to you, what you really want for yourself in the next three to six months, and what support you need to help you stay on track and achieve your vision, purpose, and goals. Good luck with your journey towards a better life.

All our dreams can come true if we dare to pursue them.
Walt Disney

IDEALIZE ROLE-MODELS

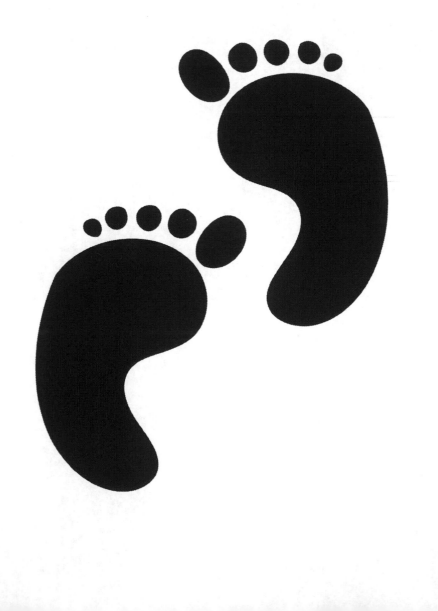

PRINCIPLE 06

IDEALIZE ROLE-MODELS

I think a role model is a mentor -
someone you see daily and learn from them.
Denzel Washington

Whatever you are trying to achieve in life, chances are higher that someone has already done it. Whoever this person is, he surely has a proven victory in your field of choice.

The surest path to being a champion is to follow the footprints of a champion. This person has *earned* the legitimate right to be your role model. Once you decide to unleash your passion, see who else has already unleashed their passion to the maximum. Following the footprints of your role model can save time, resources, and effort. Your role model can take you there faster, smoother, and sooner.

If you want to be great parents, find out a couple who have raised amazing kids. If you aim to scale Mount Everest, go to one of those climbers who surmounted it already. If you wish to produce a great movie, find out who recently won the Oscar award.

Think about your vision, purpose, and goals in life one more time. Can you hit on the names of individuals who could be your role models in those specific areas? When I first listened to an audio cassette of Jim Rohn, an inner voice whispered, "I would be willing to pay any price to be like him." I found Jim Rohn such an inspiration that he became my role model at first sight.

Can you recall people in your life that you found inspiring at *first sight*? These individuals could become role models.

WHAT IS A ROLE MODEL?

If you are given a chance to be a role model, I think you should always take it because you can influence a person's life in a positive light and that that's what I want to do. That's That it's what it' sits all about.
Tiger Woods

The term' term' role model" first appeared in <u>Robert K. Merton's Merton's</u> medical students' socialization research. Merton hypothesized that individuals compare themselves with <u>reference groups</u> of people who occupy the social role to which the individual aspires. The term has passed into general use to mean any *"person who serves as an example, whose behavior is emulated by others."*

Who is a role model? A good role model is a person who is looked up to and respected by others, inspiring others to higher achievement, someone whose behavior you believe is worthy of emulation. A role model serves as an example of positive, productive behavior.

Good role modeling begins in the home. As children, we tend to copy our parents' parents' behavior, be it good or bad, responsible, or irresponsible.

WHY ROLE MODEL?

"Everyone in society should be a role model, not only for their own self-respect but also for others."
Barry Bonds

By having role models, we can see how others live their lives and learn from their failures and successes. Rather than having to fumble around in the dark, we have a roadmap in front of us. Here are some reasons why they are so important and how you can become a role model.

No matter what you have decided to become in your life, chances are that this decision has been inspired by a role model. Something about that person attracted you, and a voice whispered in your inner ear, *"Hey, that' sthat's precisely the way I would like to be."*

What do you like to be? A sports star, a TV anchor, an entrepreneur, a movie star, a scientist, an author, a motivational speaker, a choreographer, an accountant, a lawyer, a comedian, a wrestler, a magician, a dress designer, a musician, an architect, a chef, a pilot, a philanthropist, a teacher, or a politician? You will invariably find that someone from that profession has impressed you tremendously and influenced you in its favor.

CHOOSE YOUR ROLE MODEL(s)

When you look around at the people you admire, whether parent or parental figure, sports celebrity, activist, public speaker or anyone else you feel is hugely successful, learn all you can about those persons. Do not miss the opportunity to talk with your role models directly. You can always read about them in their biographies, books, and articles or watch videos or Google them on the Internet. You will be able to discover how they got to where they are now.

1. What mistakes did they make along the way?
2. How can you use their advice or actions to influence or change your own life?
3. How can you avoid the pitfalls they encountered?

What can a role model give you? The most significant gift a role model can give is an inspiration. Whenever I think about my role models in life, I immediately start feeling enthused, stirred, stimulated, and motivated.

Since your role models have already made significant strides on life's path, they can be your guide. Even if they are not physically present to guide you, you can still learn about their life strategies by reading about them. You can emulate their best qualities and start making their character traits an integral part of your personality and your day-to-day life.

HIRE A COACH

The logical culmination of this process would be to build a coach-and-mentor relationship with your role model. This may not always be possible or practical, but if you try hard, who knows – you may build a great relationship with your role model!

Those who pluck up the courage to meet their role models, build relationships and learn from them sometimes find the opportunity to work with them or become part of projects where they can benefit from their expertise. Take sports, say cricket, where a young batsman, newly inducted into the team, eventually ends up making a record partnership with his ideal batsman who once was his role model.

Or a novice actor joins a movie in which his movie star role model is playing the lead along with him.

EXERCISE

1. Identify the areas were performing at a world-class level is indispensable to realize your purpose and passion.
2. Make a list of role models who exemplify the best in all those respective roles.
3. Choose the best role model in each category.
4. List the characteristics, traits, qualities of role models in each category.
5. Rate yourself on those traits and qualities.
6. Develop a strategy to match your role model's enthusiasm, confidence, speed, professionalism, self-belief, and skills.

Picking the right role model is enormously crucial to your career and for achieving total fulfillment in everything you do. At the same time, you have to be careful when choosing your role models: look for someone who inspires you to be the best that you can be.

Try to find a good role model or a mentor at your workplace. The influence of a good role model will significantly improve your chance of realizing your life's full potential.

Another way could be picking the top 5 people in your profession, doing thorough research on them, finding out the secrets of their success, and then creating your own action plan based on that research.

You may find your role model perfect in terms of professional skills, but you may be disappointed when you discover other aspects of his life that don't live up to your ideal.

Therefore, I suggest that you combine all the positive traits of 4-5 top personalities in your field of work and create your own list of qualities and traits you aspire to develop. An then incorporate these characteristics into your own personality.

Are you willing to give whatever it takes to become like your role model?

CONQUER FEARS

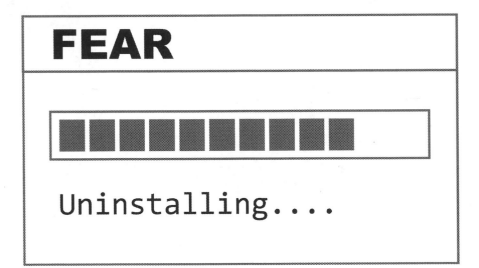

FEAR

Uninstalling....

PRINCIPLE 07

CONQUER FEARS

> *Believe in yourself, take on your challenges,*
> *dig deep within yourself to conquer fears.*
> *Never let anyone bring you down. You got to keep going.*
> *Chantal Sutherland*

The biggest obstacle on your way to success is your biggest fear. Remove the fear, and success is all yours. Failure to eliminate the fear keeps you where you are. To conquer success, conquer your fear first.

By the way, have you ever experienced fear? How does it feel to be afraid? If I ask you to make a list of your fears, what that list would include?

If you are like most of the people, you had already skipped my last question. I suggest you go back over again and make a list.

So how many items did the list include? What were the fears that you actually experienced? How frequently? What fears actually remained only fears? Can you shortlist your top three fears?

The latest research in Psychology reveals some interesting facts:

- 40% of the things we fear about never happen
- 30% are in the past and can't be helped
- 15% involve the affairs of others that are not even our business
- 12% percent relate to sickness, real or imagined.

That means 97% of our fears are irrational, unreasonable, and unnecessary. Only 3% percent of the things we fear are even likely to happen!

Curiosity will conquer fear even more than bravery will.
- James Stephens

Another shocking fact is that we are born with only two natural fears:

- *Fear of falling*
- *Fear of loud noise*

Anything else that you 'label' as fear is actually not a *pure* fear. However, since your childhood, you have expanded this list. You have allowed so many *impure* fears to become part of your list. You have been feeding these fears so long and so well that they have grown stronger.

Success depends on your ability to conquer your most robust fears.

The biggest obstacle on your way to success is your biggest fear. There would be a million definitions of what fear is. My meaning of fear is straightforward. Practical. Focused. Moreover, the meaning offers you a strategy to combat the fear as well. My definition of fear is as follows:

Fake Excuses Adjourning Results!

This definition has four parts:

Part 01: Fake:

Most of the fears we experience are not real. They are only fake. Imaginary. Non-existent. Is it right to be afraid of something unreal? If we dig deeper, we all know that our fears are baseless, forged, and bogus. Would you ever fear a fake police officer? Would you ever give in to the authority of a bogus doctor? Would you not challenge the power of a counterfeit, not? Then why to accept the power of our fake fears?

Part 02: Excuses

The best explanation of our fears is that they are sheer excuses. Nothing more. An excuse is an excuse. What else would you call it? Adding to this, the excuse is not even real. Its plain fake. Would you allow excuses to keep you from achieving what you are capable of?

Part 03: Adjourning

Now we come to the effect side. Our fears (false excuses) persuade us to delay action. Postpone pursuing our ambition. Put a halt on our effort. Procrastinate what is critical for our success. Fears frighten us so that we can put our life on a standstill mode. Terminate our efforts, break the momentum. Interrupt the flow of our actions. Fears conspire against our ability to move ahead and prove to us that taking a break is in our best interest.

Part 04: Results

The fourth part of this definition is the results. That is what defines a superstar. A champion. A true winner. However, our fears keep us from producing those results.

As our worst enemies, our fears block our way through false excuses, convincing us to choose postponement of our actions that can take us to the victory stand.

> *Fear is the primary source of superstition, and one of the main sources of cruelty. To conquer fear is the beginning of wisdom.*
> *Bertrand Russell*

Some of the most popular, most widely experienced false excuses are:

- Fear of failure
- Fear of unknown
- Fear of loss
- Fear of rejection
- Fear of losing money
- Fear of criticism
- Fear of losing a job
- Fear of inadequacy
- Fear of sickness
- Fear of success

You are not scared of the dark. You're scared of what's in it.
You're not afraid of heights. You are afraid of falling. You're not
an afraid failure. You're afraid of the feeling of worthlessness
that might bring. You are not afraid of what others think. You're

afraid of how that will make you feel. You're not afraid to try again. You're afraid of failure and of getting hurt again.
- Nancy Sathre Vogle

THE ANTIDOTE OF FEAR

It is not the mountain we conquer but ourselves.
Edmund Hillary

The shortest story to combat fear:

'Fear knocked on the door. Love got up to see who it was. Love opened the door. There was no one outside'.

Every day, almost without failing, fear knocks our doors. Most of us go for two choices:

CHOICE #1:

When we hear fear knocking the door, we feel so terrified. We don't dare open the door. Something within tells us we won't be able to handle fear. We better hide. So we choose to avoid it. We pretend as if we didn't hear the knock. We invent reasons for not opening the door.

We postpone action. We confine ourselves to that dark room of inaction. We let the fear mark a boundary around our comfort zone. Our sense of safety increases. (and the sense of achievement decreases). We confine ourselves. We get trapped by comfort. We choose to give up on the dreams outside this zone of comfort. We limit ourselves.

But the comfort turns out to be an eyewash. It was an illusion, comfort actually hands us over to discomfort. We feel suffocated, and helplessness begins to prevail. We shout for help.

CHOICE #2:

We hear the fear knocking. We get terrified. We choose to battle with fear. We talk a stock of our preparation against fear. We send anger to battle with fear. Anger is powerful. Aggressive. Furious. Ready to combat.

Anger attacks fear. First, our anger assaults fear with verbal attacks. Fear equals that with much more intensity. Then the one-on-one fight begins. Both anger and fear are skillful, powerful, and harmful. However, anger loses the battle.

Result: we are pushed back to our comfort circle. Confined. Defeated. Limited. Fears gain more power. We feel more terrified.

Fear roars outside the door of our comfort. Challenging us. We refuse to accept the challenge. We decide to never wrestle with our fear again. We accept our inadequacy to combat. Our belief in being weak further strengthens. We live the rest of our life within the confinement of our own limiting thoughts and feelings.

THE RIGHT CHOICE

We all know two realities:

1. Avoiding fear is not wise.
2. Using anger to 'fight' with fear is not useful.

So what is the right choice? The story reveals the one million dollar lesson:

Fear cannot face love. Fear is afraid of love. Fear doesn't dare to contest love. Therefore, whenever you sense the knock of fear at the door of your potential, never avoid it. Face it. But with love. Not with anger.

What is facing fear with love?

Facing fear with love means, using your passion for outfighting fear. Love means what you feel passionate about. Something you love doing. Passion and love represent the heart. (remember chapter two?). When we genuinely love what we aim to do, no matter how terrified we feel, passion always wins. The size of our passion is always more significant than the size of fear. Love outsizes fear. Always. No questions about it.

Love and fear cannot co-exist in one heart. In your heart, either you can accumulate love of what you really want to accomplish or fear of not accomplishing it.

The problem is that when fear knocks the door, we get paralyzed. We forget our real power to face fear – love.

Fear knocks you down because you miss the recipe. What is the recipe? Fear and love cannot co-exist. Whichever you focus first, imprison you. So hard that you cannot even think of the other one.

So next time, you hear a knock, stay calm. Don't panic. Smile inside you. You know how to handle the knock. Take a pause. Ask, anger to sit down. No need to waste time in 'verbal boxing.' Why wasting your arsenal fighting. Call your love. Open the door with belief. You will meet no one inside.

Fear has never been seen by anyone. The truth is it doesn't exist. Anywhere. It resides only in your mind.

FACE YOUR FEARS

If you do not conquer self, you will be conquered by self.
- Napoleon Hill

Once upon a time, inland for away, there lives an enormous giant. He was at least ten feet tall, with a mop of red hair and beard, and in his hand, he carried a mighty ax.

Every year, on the same day, at the same time, the giant would walk down from the mountains, which were his home, to stand outside the castle walls, terrorizing the inhabitants.

'Come, send me your bravest man, and I will fight him, 'the giant would shout, towering over the wall and waving his ax menacingly. *'Send me someone to fight, or I will knock down your castle walls and kill everyone with my ax. Every* year, the gate in the castle wall would open slowly and fearfully, and one poor, valiant soul would walk out to face and certain death.

'Is this the best you can do?' the giant would laugh mockingly. The poor wretch would stand, mesmerized by the enormity of the giant and the task in hand. Not one person had even managed to draw his sword before the giant would crush them with his mighty fist and chop them into tiny pieces with his ax.

But then one day, a young prince arrived in the town. *'Why does everyone here look so frightened and sad?'* he asked a fellow traveler.

'You haven't seen the giant? Replied the traveler

'What giant? Asked the young prince, intrigued

The traveler told him the tale.

'Every year, on this very day, the giant arrived and challenged our braves to a duel. And every year, he stays them exactly where they stand. They don't even move to draw their swords. It's as though the giant hypnotizes them.'

'We'll see about them,' said the young prince.

When the giant arrived later that day, he was waiting for him.

'Come send me your bravest man, and I will fight him, the giant shouted.

'I am here, said the young prince,* throwing open the gate and striding out toward him.

For a moment, they stood and face each other. Although the giant was still a long way away from him, the young prince was instantly struck by the sheer size and shocking appearance of his opponent.

But, summoning up all his courage, he started to walk toward the giant, brandishing his sword, and never taking his eyes off that dreadful face with the red hair and red beard.

Suddenly, he realized that as he was walking, the giant - rather than appearing larger – actually began to shrink before his very eyes. He stopped and stared. The giant was only five feet tall.

He walked closer to him, still then stopped and stared. Now the giant was only two feet tall. He continued walking until he was face to face with the giant, and each step the prince took, he saw the giant shrink. By now, the giant was so small that he looked up at the young prince. He was only 12 inches tall.

The young prince took his sword and plunged it into the giant's heart. As the giant lay dying on the ground, the young prince bent down and whispered to him:

'Who are you?'

With his dying breath, the giant replied, *'my name is Fear.'*

When you believe in yourself, choose to take action and run into your most frightening fear – the fear disappears!

> *Inaction breeds doubt and fear. Action breeds confidence and courage. If you want to conquer fear, do not sit home and think about it. Go out and get busy.*
> *Dale Carnegie*

KILL EXCUSES

KILL EXCUSES

> *Ninety-nine percent of the failures come from people who have the habit of making excuses.*
> *- George Washington Carver*

Once a farmer found an abandoned eagle's nest, and in it was an egg still warm. He took the egg back to his farm and laid it in the nest of one of his hens. The egg hatched, and the baby eagle grew up along with the other chickens.

It pecked about the farmyard, scrabbling for grain. It spent its life within the yard and rarely looked up. When it was very old, one day, it lifted up its head and saw above it a beautiful sight - an eagle soaring high above in the sky.

Looking at it, the old creature sighed and said to itself, *"If only I'd been born an eagle."*

Source: *an adaptation from an Anthony de Mello story*

What is your excuse for not living the life that you were born to live?

Like the lost eagle, do you wish to be a person that you already are? Do you have an idea who you were meant to be?

What do you want to be? Who do you want to fly like? What is stopping you from being all that you possibly can? What will take for you to recognize your genuine talent, skill, and ability?

At the core of all your justifications, explanations, and validations is an excuse.

So my next question is:

Why are you not flying higher? Why are you not soaring above? Why are you not joining the high flyers club that you actually belong to? Want me to be blunter?

So tell me, what is your excuse for not claiming your greatness?

WHAT IS AN EXCUSE?

"To rush into explanations is always a sign of weakness."
— Agatha Christie, The Seven Dials Mystery

An excuse is a limiting thought. A restraining belief. An off-putting idea. Excuse builds imaginary walls between you and your goal. Allowing you to hide so that you are no more required to take action. Excuse creates an easy way out for you so that you can avoid putting in the effort.

In reality, the attitudes, beliefs, and thoughts that support excuses do not serve you. Like it or not, it is your favorite excuse standing in your way to living your most magnificent life. Excuses are really good at opening doors of useless, and never-ending sufferings on you.

WHY EXCUSES?

"The only thing standing between you and your goal is the bullshit story you keep telling yourself as to why you can't achieve it."
— *Jordan Belfort*

'I know what to do. I recognize the benefits of doing it. I know the price of not doing it. I have the competence and resources to do it. But I still don't move an inch.'

Does this story sound familiar? We all use excuses to justify our inaction. We hide behind excuses to postpone what is critical for our success. We cannot control what happens to us, but we can *always* exercise control over how it will impact us. We do not have to let excuses drive our actions to defeat.

Excuses are damaging. Extremely self-destructive. If that is the case, then why do we keep them so close to our hearts? Why our excuses are so dear to us?

Instead of taking a stand for our dreams, why do we choose to take a stand for our excuses? Why do we fight for them? Defend them?

Bad excuses are worse than none.
- Thomas Fuller

Why do we do that?

Reason # 01:
IGNORANCE

Excuses are always disguised. They never show up in their real get up. Therefore, we fail to recognize them. We don't even know we are using excuses. We have no idea how to spot or identify excuses. We don't have the ability to discern between a genuine reason and a lame excuse. Since we don't recognize them, excuses find no problem hurting us.

Reason # 02:
NO IDEA OF COST

Excuses are free. Most of us are self-reliant in manufacturing excuses. We are factories for producing excuses. Our diseased thinking persuades us to accept excuses as free gifts. However, we fail to realize that excuses are very expensive. We don't get a hint of the cost that we might end up paying for those free excuses.

Reason # 03:
NO TOOLS TO KILL EXCUSES

We all are vulnerable to *excuse bombs.* If left unattended, these excuse bombs can explode. Devastating our dreams, aspirations, and hopes.

The price we pay for the blasts is enormous. Would you allow an excuse bomb to destroy your future? Certainly not.

It is your personal responsibility to know how to:

- Identify excuse bombs in various areas of your life.
- Diffuse excuse bombs with skill and confidence without hurting yourself

- Prevent yourself against any excuse bombs in the future. This requires shutting down all excuse manufacturing facilities.

Determination gives you the resolve to keep going in spite of the Excuses that lay before you.
- Denis Waitley

THE CONSPIRACY

When you seek the presence of your creative Spirit and are filled with passion about virtually everything you undertake, you'll successfully remove the Excuses from your life and enjoy the active presence of Spirit.
- Wayne Dyer

Have you experienced a lack of progress despite a good start?

You were ashamed of your lack of progress. You lag far behind on the goals you should have accomplished by now. What is holding you back? What is it that doesn't allow you to be all that you can be? What is it that is sapping your energy and sucking your lifeblood?

The truth is that there is a group of conspirators working against you. The members of this group do not want you to succeed. They have joined forces to stop you, no matter what it takes. Who are they? They work under a gang called 'excuses.'

I call them Excuses also because they act indirectly rather than facing you head-on, though some may have the audacity to do so. These Excuses gang up on you and work every day to deprive you of some of your precious productive time.

These excuses conspire against you in different ways to make your plans fail. Their planning usually kills your plans. You remain where you were when you first started (*sometimes for years*). You don't move forward even an inch.

FOCUS ON GOALS, NOT EXCUSES

Do the thing you fear to do and keep on doing it... that is the quickest and surest way ever yet discovered to conquer fear.
Dale Carnegie

After putting so much effort into developing your purpose, vision, and goals, I am sure you would not like to see your efforts going down the drain. The most significant risk you face in your life's journey is losing focus, getting distracted, and not being able to start.

Whether it is a sports stadium or cutthroat competition in the business world, it is a focus that determines the outcome. Greater focus will yield greater rewards. Loss of focus will result in a total loss.

Focus can help you stay on the success track. If you go off-track, no matter how hard you try or how fast you run, you will end up nowhere. This journey will take you through various routes, paths, tunnels, past hazards, and down rugged trails. You will be challenged to maintain your pace and focus. You will undoubtedly make mistakes on your way. Making mistakes is no big deal, but you will have to learn how to quickly switch your focus from the mistake of developing methods to ensure you do not make the same mistake again.

Success is never a smooth ride. The barriers may appear unconquerable, but remember no obstacle lasts permanently. When you focus on what you want, you do whatever it takes to get there. When you lose your way, but the focus back where it belongs. If you have a bigger goal, be ready for a bigger disappointment. Why? The higher the value of the goal, the higher is the price.

Retain a sharp focus on your destination. On the way, you can encounter a hostile crowd, an unfair umpire, bad luck, or a critical decision going against you. The spotlight will either focus on what has gone wrong or what can still be improved upon.

If you focus on negative things, you will become a negative person.

Goals need sustained effort. Make progress, build momentum, and follow through till you achieve. Life offers you multiple opportunities and options. It is, therefore, essential for you to choose paths, people, and activities that help you reach the destination you envisioned.

THE STRATEGY

"I do not believe in excuses. I believe in hard work as the prime solvent of life's problems". - James Cash Penney

- Find out where you are at right now.
- How different is this place from where you want to be? Is this place closer or farther away from your desired destination?
- What will happen if you continue to invent excuses?

EXPOSING EXCUSES

I do not believe in excuses. I believe in hard work
as the prime solvent of life's problems.
- James Cash Penney

The first step in killing excuses is to unmask them. *Excuses* are not very easy to unveil. Since it is difficult to expose them, they continue to damage us as distracters, exhausters, and speed breakers.

Have you ever made a serious effort to expose excuses? Are you ready to pinpoint and catch some of them right now? If you are, I can share a no-fail plan with you.

Step #01:
BUILD YOUR EXCUSE DIRECTORY:

Put all the excuses on a piece of paper. Major or minor, shrewd or naive, visible or disguised, old or new, favorite or compulsory, borrowed from others or your own inventions, robust or easy to handle, known to you or unknown to you. Put them all down on a sheet of paper. See how the list looks like?

How do you feel about your list?

> *It is wise to direct your anger towards problems - not people; to focus your energies on answers - not excuses.*
> *- William Arthur Ward*

Step #02:
SPOT EXCUSES

My thousands of coaching hours with all kinds of people reveal a stunning truth: given a choice, most of us will fail to *spot* our most cunning excuses. To make this process easy for you, I am presenting the most widely used *excuse directory* to you.

The list includes some of the most dangerous, notorious, and treacherous excuses of all times. These excuses have destroyed millions of lives and trillions of dreams.

Please take a look at the list carefully. You may not have considered these statements as excuses previously. Knowing what you are about to know now, you will not underestimate the negative power of excuses hidden within these statements.

YOUR EXCUSE DIRECTORY

1. It is too dangerous.'
2. It is not going to be fair
3. This is beyond my reach
4. I don't need to over-stretch myself
5. I will look awkward
6. No one has time to help me
7. It's against my nature
8. I don't have that much time to wait.'
9. My family will never agree
10. I won't be able to afford that
11. I don't have the stamina
12. Rules of the game will go against me
13. At least I am better
14. Don't you see it is too harsh.'
15. It is so time taking
16. Someone like me cannot get that
17. I don't have the power
18. I am frightened
19. No one has ever done it before
20. There is no one to support me
21. I don't have time
22. I am not as smart as others
23. I am too old for this
24. My family was ... ...
25. I am too young for this
26. It's beyond what I can handle
27. I have no resources
28. I am so tired

29. It is not practical
30. I am ok with what I have
31. Who cares?
32. Why me?

> *Leadership - leadership is about taking*
> *responsibility, not making excuses.*
> *- Mitt Romney*

How many excuses have you been able to expose? How do you feel about the list? Shocked? Guilty? Furious? Fooled?

Did you spot the ones you have been using naively? How many of them were manufactured in your own factory?

Step #03:
ARREST & INVESTIGATE

Let go of the disempowering feelings. Enjoy the power you have gained on your most taxing excuses. The ones that polluted your motivation, damaged your reputation, and delayed your greatness.

Celebrate the victory over them. But before you arrest them, throw them in jail, imprison them for a lifetime or put them in solitary confinement; you need to complete the investigation below:

1. How long have you been using these excuses?
2. What damage have they already done to you?
3. What professional growth opportunities have you already missed because of them?
4. How these excuses have hampered your personal development?

5. What is the estimation of the overall cost of being trapped by these excuses?
6. Where did you take these excuses from?
7. Who has been *financing* these excuses? You or others?
8. Which one of these is your most troublesome, hard-hitting, and painful excuses? You may pick up the top five.

Step #04:
PUNISH & HANG EXCUSES

The excuses deserve no mercy. You must punish them in a way that sets an example.

So what strategy is your strategy to ensure that these excuses never dare to rob your energy, focus, and sense of achievement again?

Be totally committed to this process. Be hard, ruthless, brutal, pitiless, and hard-nosed. Don't spare them, don't forgive them. No matter how much they plead, don't let them off the hook; hold them to account.

Punishing excuses can be a painful task. Most of these excuses will disclose a strong connection with *you*. Once you launch an impartial investigation, your own reputation, credibility, and competence can come under attack. You will have to embrace the pain, as it cannot all be avoided. However, you are left with two choices:

1. Embrace the pain of discipline
2. Embrace the pain of regret

My coach Jim Rohn says, '*The pain of discipline weighs in ounces, whereas the pain of regret weighs in tons.*'

Which pain would you choose for yourself?

In one of my success seminars, a CEO of a global FMCG almost shrieked, *"I have identified the enemy, yes, I've spotted him."*

"Who on earth is the enemy?" the entire group screamed back.

"I have identified the enemy," the CEO repeated, shocked, *"and it is me!"*

Who is your enemy? What is stopping you from becoming all that you possibly can?

Let me put it another way:

'What would you do differently if you knew you only had six more months to live?'

'What are you waiting for? What's stopping you from doing it now?'

> *If you're trying to achieve, there will be roadblocks. I've had them; everybody has had them. But obstacles don't have to stop you. If you run into a wall, don't turn around and give up. Figure out how to climb it, go through it, or work around it.*
> *- Michael Jordan*

DISCIPLINE YOURSELF

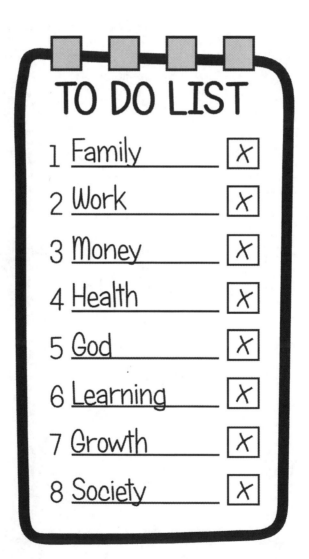

DISCIPLINE YOURSELF

> *"Self-discipline is often disguised as short-term pain, which often leads to long-term gains. The mistake many of us make is the need and want for short-term gains (immediate gratification), which often leads to long-term pain."*
> — Charles F. Glassman, Brain Drain The Breakthrough That Will Change Your Life

Sharing Tick Tick Dollar philosophy and principles is one of the most rewarding experiences in my life. I enjoy it primarily because of the significant transitions in thinking and behavior that I witness in people during my sessions. Participants who are initially perplexed, defensive, and resistant to change gradually start accepting ideas and thoughts very different from what they had believed to be accurate.

When I teach self-discipline, the most frequent comment participant share is, 'I try to discipline myself. However, I rarely manage to achieve all the goals I was supposed to by the end of my workday. Despite my best efforts, there's hardly a day that all gets done.'

When you want to do more and think there is not enough time during the day, you start to feel pressured. This pressure leads to an imbalance. You start eating into energy and effort that has been allotted to another essential part of your life. This imbalance produces a feeling of dissatisfaction that later on converts into stress.

But why can't you get everything done during your workday in the first place? You get bogged down in dozens of unnecessary, unwanted and unproductive activities. We all continue throwing our valuable minutes, hours, and days into a '*time drain*'.

Is 'self-discipline a fairytale? Is *getting it all done really possible?* Why do we end up accomplishing only a tiny fraction of what we '*could have*' done?

The plain and simple fact is that people will measure your performance only by what you finish in the business. Nobody counts what you have left undone. People will always leave undone far more than they ever accomplish. If our organizations, clients, bosses, customers, and everyone else is expecting us to do it ALL and can't, where should we focus?

My answer is simple:

1. Don't focus on what does not get done (*at least for the time being*). Take pride in whatever you have been able to accomplish during the day. If you overthink what was left *undone,* you are bound to feel discouraged.
2. Devise a strategy to direct your focus each day to what is truly important to you, your organization, and your business.

This two-step solution will help you stay motivated (because you are acknowledging your own efforts) and make you more productive (as you are turning your attention away from the problem to focus on the solution).

> *A self-discipline is an act of cultivation. It requires you to connect today's actions to tomorrow's results. There's a season for sowing a season for reaping. Self-discipline helps you know which is which.*
> Gary Ryan Blair

DISCIPLINE TOOLS

Self-discipline is a tough subject to master. No self-discipline is possible without self-organization. Don't make a mess of your life. Take full responsibility for whatever is lacking in your life. Use the tools available in this book to organize yourself to go even beyond its boundaries. Find out what works best for you, create your own tools, and transform the life of your imagination into a living reality.

"The first and best victory is to conquer self."
— Plato
Greek Philosopher

DAA WAA MAA YAA

Law of DAA WAA MAA YAA helps you bring discipline to your life. It allows you to build bridges between your purpose, passion, and whatever you do on a day to day basis.

DAA: Day Arranged in Advance
WAA: Week Arranged in Advance
MAA: Month Arranged in Advance
YAA: Year Arranged in Advance

In one of my training workshops, a participant stood up and asked, *'Why don't you add LAA to the process?'*

'What does this LAA stand for?' I asked curiously.

'Life Arranged in Advance,' he said, smiling.

Are you willing to give it a try?

DAILY INTENSITY

> *We all have dreams. But to make dreams come into reality, it takes an awful lot of determination, dedication, self-discipline, and effort.*
> *Jesse Owens*

I asked one of my friends, *'Do you go for daily planning every day?"* He replied, *'Only if I want to have a good day.'* Without a plan executed with daily intensity, you are often side-tracked to the things that are easier to accomplish, or drawn to the most essential items.

ONE NIGHT BEFORE

Do you wish to effectively control your most precious resource, the next twenty-four hours of your life? Plan your next day one night before. That planning will help you focus on the most critical aspects of your day and enhance your productivity.

DATE DATE DATE:
Every Document

Every time you write something on a new piece of paper, start with the date. Why? Because after several days, weeks, or months, you will have difficulty remembering the context. What does a date tell you? Everything, especially the frame of reference, and exactly how much time has passed.

LAW OF HPO
(Handle Paper Once)

A paper should be handled only once. No procrastination, no delays, one paper at a time. Is it okay for a business executive to bury himself in a landslide of paperwork?

I was surprised when I discovered that an average person receives around 250 communications each day via email, telephone, fax, paper mail, memos, circulars, and multiple social media channels (*Facebook, LinkedIn, etc.*).

Paper handling is such an unnecessary problem. A lot of time is wasted going through the same pile of papers day after day and correcting mistakes when things slip through the cracks. Try to handle the paper just once and be done with it.

> *With self-discipline most anything is possible.*
> *Theodore Roosevelt*

PRACTICE UJF
(Ugliest Job First)

UJF is an animating principle. An *'ugly job'* is something you do not take much interest in, or something intricate and complex. An ugly job should also be worthy of being placed on a top priority list.

STANDARDIZE:
The Routine Tasks

If you are required to perform a few jobs as a matter of routine, develop some SOP or system. This will ensure you do not miss any critical step. Successful businesses and organizations have systems in place for handling each goal. If you are involved in doing something that is of a recurring nature, think about developing a system to handle repetitive tasks. *'Stop reinventing the wheel and recreating the same things over and again.'*

BUS SYSTEM
(Back-Up System)

Have you ever lost your cell phone and consequently lost all your contacts? Have you also suffered because of computer problems that resulted in a loss of relevant information and documents?

You realize the importance of protecting your data, but you are so busy that you don't have the time to do it. Organized people, on the other hand, will never suffer a loss of data. They always have a *Back-Up System (BUS)*. The most effective system includes:

Grandmother Copy: *(every year)*
Mother Copy: *(every quarter)*
Daughter Copy: *(every week)*

PIN PRINCIPLE:
Practice Intelligent Neglect

When you have *too much to do* and *too little time* to do it, then you can choose to intelligently neglect a few things to reduce the pressure on your time.

SOCIALIZE LESS

Avoid becoming a social butterfly. Making friends and developing a network of professional relationships is all right, but spending too much time on the phone, text messaging, emailing, *Facebooking*, etc. can drain your productivity.

COLLABORATE

Long gone is the time when you were required to compete against others. Our current era is all about *collaboration*. Cooperation from fellow workers, colleagues, and peers can make your life so much easier. Develop your list of personal contacts, your networking list, on an on-going basis. Always offer to help everyone on your list whenever you can.

MAJOR IN MINORS?

Investing your energy in tasks that don't offer a high pay-off is majoring in minor things. Save your best talents, skills, and abilities for the most important goals of your life. Don't waste them on trivial, insignificant, petty tasks. Majoring in minor subjects will offer you no pay off.

BALANCE

The best organizing tool available on earth is balancing your work and family life. You can find creative opportunities to bring your work and family closer and succeed on both fronts.

ESCAPE THE MEETINGS TRAP

The easiest way to deal with meetings is to ask yourself and the others involved, *'Is this meeting really essential?'* Another question that can be even more helpful is, *'Am I really required to attend this meeting?'*

ONE ITEM

> *In reading the lives of great men, I found that the first victory they won was over themselves... self-discipline with all of them came first.*
> *Harry S Truman*

If you are easily disturbed by environmental distractions, let me share a surprising secret of how to complete tasks. (*I, for one, am not easily distracted. I have trained my mind to remain focused on the goal. Even while multitasking, I do not allow distractions to disrupt my concentration.*)

Let's get back to the solution. If you are inclined to be easily distracted, work with one thing in front of you at a time so that other things will not distract you. You can use that old aphorism '*out of sight, out of mind*' to your advantage.

BIT BY BIT

If a task seems gigantic, don't see it as oversized. You can always break it down into little bite-size, manageable pieces. Once you take the first step and get the task started, you will be surprised to discover how soon it will be completed.

WAR
(Within Arm's Reach)

A lot of your time is wasted on accessing or finding things—people throw-away an inordinate amount of time searching for things that should be within arm's reach.

Staplers, scales, sharpeners, printers, scanners, and other crucial items that you need frequently should be kept handy. Otherwise, you will leave your workstation in search of a stapler and return after losing twenty minutes on superfluous chit-chat going on somewhere in the office.

POWER OF THE PEN

Use your mind for the bigger picture, and a pen to elaborate on the details. This is one of the most useful tools I have ever discovered. As a consultant, I have developed the habit of taking notes during client meetings. Whenever I go back to the same client or make some decisions, I always refer to my notes to refresh my memory. This helps me in negotiating more effectively and being better prepared for the meeting.

DISCIPLINING YOUR PLANS

*"Once you have a commitment, you need the
discipline and hard work to get you there."*
Haile Gebrselassie

Disciplining yourself is not possible if you don't know where your plans and time is draining out. If you don't keep proper track of your time, you will never accomplish anything.

Have you ever had a few hours left over on a Sunday night and decided to use them during the next week? Making the decision was easy enough but did you find this *inter-week transfer* easy? You would have doubtless discovered that the 52-week network has not yet started offering a '*transfer*' facility.

You get only 24 hours in a day and a total of 168 hours per week. There is no savings bank account for time. You can either spend time or waste of time. And when you decide to spend it, you have limited options. You can spend your time wisely – or unwisely.

If you make a careful assessment, you will be shocked to discover that two to three hours vanish down the drain every day. Where does this time go? Who steals this from you without you even noticing? What is this '*time drain*'?

It's all down to what you can call '*useless disturbances*'.

Tracking your time will allow you to distinguish between a positive disturbance and a contrary disturbance. Can a disturbance be positive? Yes, why not. Anything that reduces your ability to achieve a crucial goal is a harmful disturbance, while something that empowers you to accomplish a much-needed goal is a positive disturbance.

When a fellow team member enters your room uninvited and shares a piece of information you badly need or gets a vital business tip during the interaction, don't you think it is a positive disturbance? What about a customer who calls to place a big order for your products? Surely that is a positive disturbance?

But if your team member uses up the same amount of your time to complain or discuss things unrelated to the business, that is unquestionably a complete wastage of time. That is time lost down the drain.

Would you like to know more about this '*time drain*'? Time tracking is the answer.

Tracking your plans against time will permit you to discover some significant findings. For example, have you noticed how many times you get interrupted in a typical workday? Research shows that if you combine both human and technological interruptions, a person gets disturbed approximately 50 times a day, six to seven times an hour. Isn't that pretty drastic?

How much time then does a disturbance use up? Some disturbances last for hours and some for mere seconds. On average, it's not less than five minutes. Now 50 interruptions multiplied by 5 minutes adds up to a staggering *'time drain'*, don't you feel? To be precise, it is about 50% of your total workday, four solid hours!

I hope you realize now how important it is to keep track of your time. Tracking time will also tell you that very few of these disturbances are impacting your work achievements positively.

TRACKING GUIDELINES

> *"Success is nothing more than a few simple disciplines, practiced every day." Jim Rohn*

The most effective way to discipline yourself is to keep track of where your time is going. One of the most effective methods is the time log. It offers you the opportunity to trace exactly where your time has gone. How a time log helps you:

– A time log is useful for auditing time. It gives you an honest and transparent assessment of the way you use your time.

– It helps you analyze how you *actually* spend your time against what you planned.

– If you look carefully, a time log will pinpoint your best and worst times of the day.

– A time log will also help track changes in your energy, alertness, and effectiveness levels.

– Best of all, a time log will identify and eliminate time-wasting or low-yield tasks.

> *By constant self-discipline and self-control,*
> *you can develop greatness of character.*
> *– Grenville Kleiser*

Using a time log also requires discipline. I suggest you use the time log for at least a week. You will automatically discover the logic of continuing this practice after that. After one week, based on the information collected through the time log, you can run a weekly analysis by placing it into four categories. You can call them the 4 Cs of tracking:

1. CATEGORIZE:

Pick some relevant categories to cover all your possible uses of time. The categories could include job/paid work, home and family, study and personal development, unpaid or voluntary work, sleep, watching TV, and other recreational activities, maintenance, personal care.

2. CHOOSE

Decide the amount of time you would choose to spend on each of them. For instance, how much time you would allocate to voluntary work in a given week.

3. CHECK:

The third stage is for a reality check. Use the time log to check what is happening in reality. Does the actual time you spent on a category match with your original plans?

4. CHANGE:

The discrepancies between steps 2 and 3 will give you enough material to ponder on. *'Change'* is indeed a call for action. It serves as a wake-up call and demands an instant commitment to effecting a change in the state of affairs.

Taking this analysis one step forward, you should immediately take two actions:

1. Eliminate jobs that your employer shouldn't be paying you to do.
2. Reduce the amount of time spent on personal tasks

Time tracking is a significant milestone in your journey to create a prosperous and successful life. Then why would you even consider *not* using it? Sure, you have excuses. The most frequent excuses I come across are:

1. *I was too busy.*
2. *It seems a waste of time.*
3. *I missed a day and gave up.*
4. *I felt guilty because it showed me clearly how much time I was wasting.*

If you are overcome by excuses, think about the following benefits of time tracking:

- You can recognize the BLACK HOLES.
- You can conduct a lost time analysis.

- You can identify and understand time loss patterns.
- You can figure out your most productive time.
- You can identify your least productive time.

Don't underestimate the significance of time tracking and the utilization of a time log. You will only be able to truly appreciate all the multiple benefits once you use these tools. Don't skip a step – withstand any temptation to resistance, no matter how strong it is. Take the first step, move ahead, and reap the rewards of time tracking.

RECIPE FOR DISASTER

I have shared with you a variety of tools designed to multiply success and achieve affluence. How come you still do not care enough about accelerating results to achieve prosperity, success, and fulfillment?

If you are seriously unwilling or reluctant to utilize these tools, including the 10 accelerators mentioned above, I can offer you the *perfect recipe* for making your life absolutely miserable and losing everything you have achieved so far. Below is a time-tested formula that guarantees a disastrous life:

1. Never say No
2. Promise a lot
3. Never plan your time
4. Clutter up your office
5. Chuck your watch into a garbage can
6. Don't schedule your activities
7. Live a goalless life
8. Invite interruptions
9. Live in a state of perpetual emergency
10. Don't act, *just chill*

How do you like the recipe? It works amazingly fast. But I do not recommend that you try it.

> *A dream doesn't become a reality through magic;*
> *it takes sweat, determination, and hard work.*
> *- Colin Powell*

OVER DELIVER

PRINCIPLE 10

OVER DELIVER

> Success is finding satisfaction in giving a little more than you take.
> Christopher Reeve

World-class performers always mesmerize their audience with their performance. Why? They over-deliver. They always aim to deliver more than what anyone else could expect of them.

Their client expectations do not drive them. They raise the bar by putting high expectations on them. And then they do everything possible to exceed those expectations.

WHAT IS OVER-DELIVER?

SET HIGH STANDARDS

In this Principle, you will learn some fundamental and exceedingly essential lessons about organizing yourself that can increase your productivity in a big way.

EXPECT MORE FROM YOURSELF

You can only over-deliver if you expect the most from yourself.

GO EXTRA MILES

I read somewhere 'there are no traffic jams at the extra mile.' Make sure you go a little extra so that people remember you for your extraordinary performance.

BE WORLD CLASS

Either you aim to be genuinely world-class at what you do or just leave the filed.

BE A GIVER

Don't focus on what you get. Just focus on what you can give. Life gives to the givers and takes from the takers.

KNOW WHO IS OFFERING WHAT?

Remember, all principles in this part of the book are connected to one metaphor – scoreboard. Before you begin the quest to over-deliver, you need to know who is delivering your field. What score have the others already put on the board? If you are unaware of their score, how would you know you have already beaten them?

LEAVE YOUR MARK. WORK IS IDENTITY.

In my belief, work is not a way to earn money. It's a way to mark your identity on everything you do. It means leaving your signature, leaving a legacy behind you.

OVER-DELIVER MINDSET

What does it take to over-deliver?

WILLINGNESS

Ready to go beyond the call of duty.

CUSTOMER FOCUS

A sharper focus on whoever is watching you play, i.e., customers, classmates, teammates, teachers, media, etc.

SERVICE ORIENTATION

When you bring a sincere sense of service orientation in all you do, people instantly become fans of your passion.

CREATIVITY AND ORIGINALITY

Delivering beyond expectations becomes a reality when you are creative and innovative. When you devote yourself to find solutions. When you promise to be original.

PINO FACTOR

Don't let the PINO Factor impact you negatively. Make sure that achieved results always reflect your positive intent.

PINO stands for:

Positive
Intent
No
Outcome

TOOLS TO OVER-DELIVER

1. SHARPENING THE SAW

Once upon a time, there were two woodcutters named Peter and John. They were often at loggerheads over who chopped more wood. So one day, they decided to hold a competition to determine the winner. The rules were simple—whoever produces the most wood in a day wins.

So the next morning, both of them took up their positions in the forest and started chopping away in their fastest possible speed. This lasted for an hour before Peter suddenly stopped. When John realized that there was no chopping sound from his opponent's side, he thought: "Ah Ha! He must be tired already!" And he continued to cut down his trees with double the pace.

A quarter of an hour passed, and John heard his opponent chopping again. So both of them carried on synchronously. John was starting to feel weary when the chopping from Peter stopped once again. Feeling motivated and smelling victory close by, John continued, with a smile on his face.

This went on the whole day. Every hour, Peter would stop chopping for fifteen minutes while John kept going relentlessly. So when the competition ended, John was confident that he would take the triumph.

But to John's astonishment, Peter had cut down more wood. How did this even happen? "How could you have chopped down more trees than me? I heard you stop working every hour for fifteen minutes!", exclaimed John.

Peter replied, "Well, it's straightforward. Every time I stopped work, while you were still chopping down trees, I sharpened my ax."

Everybody everywhere seems to be busy. Most people are just too busy doing and trying to achieve that; they do not take the necessary time to renew themselves, learn and grow, and sharpen the "axe".

We overwork ourselves amidst the overwhelming tasks at hand. We feel drained, exhausted, and our productivity declines.

Do we simply take a break, rest, and relax? That isn't sharpening the ax—that's just putting the ax down. The blade will still be dull after your break. Yes, the woodcutter needs to rest, but only when he sharpens his blade, learns new techniques, trains up his strength and stamina, and becomes more productive.

2. FOUR POINT SCHEDULE

When preparing the schedules for the day, keep a few essential points in mind:

1: Develop the habit of working out a simple '*things to do*' list every day. This master list should include everything you would *like to* or *have to* do on a typical day.
2: Carefully evaluate every item on your list. This review should be based on some assessment questions for each item on the list. For example, does this activity ensure the best use of my time? Is there a better or more efficient way of handling or completing the task? Is there anything I can do in advance to prepare for it?
3: Keep an eye on the outcome, not the activity alone. Instead of immediately agreeing to an appointment that involves a

three-hour back and forth drive from your office, ask yourself (and the others involved) *'Can this goal be achieved through an email or a telephone call?'*

4: Put some tick marks on the most critical items on the list and do them first.

Daily scheduling and planning are the *only* available tools to help you get the most from your time and enhance your daily productivity.

3. URGENT AND IMPORTANT

One of my favorite management experts, Stephen Covey, author of *"The 7 Habits of Highly Effective People"*, has defined the distinction between urgent and vital in a brilliant way. Almost every time management book spells out this difference. Let me make it even simpler for you. Try to feel the difference between what is Urgent and what is merely Important.

URGENT: An incident, situation, task, or thing that seeks your instant awareness can be classified as 'urgent.' Essential items are deadline-driven. They are often associated with the achievement of someone else's goals. The activities are very demanding in the hunt for prompt action.

IMPORTANT: An incident, situation, task, or thing that can positively impact your *'big picture'* or overall effectiveness is 'important.' The outcome leads to the achievement of your goals.

1. Urgent-unimportant
2. Urgent-important
3. Not urgent-important
4. Not urgent-not important

Now let's pay closer attention to each one of these four classifications:

URGENT-UNIMPORTANT

These are classic time wasters. You are performing these tasks to please others. In the pursuit of these tasks, you become what Stephen Covey calls a *'public pleaser.'* This category includes annoyances, interruptions, unwanted phone calls, and tasks with no returns. People investing in this category will get no return on their investment.

Your resources will be depleted, and so will your fate. You will become a victim of self-deception because you think the tasks you are involved in are vital, whereas they are just urgent. After spending some time in this category, you will feel you have become a doormat, being used by others with no pay-off.

URGENT-IMPORTANT

This category is best described as *'crisis.'* Why? Because most items in the urgent-important category are crises. This category is filled with crucial goals, along with scary deadlines. It is characterized by burning issues, problems, dilemmas, and setbacks.

People living in this category spend most of their time fire fighting and battling immense pressure. When you handle tasks at the last moment, mediocre performance is the only outcome. Spending too much time living with stress and anxiety takes you to a stage where burnout is inevitable.

NOT URGENT-IMPORTANT

These are critical activities, but without a critical deadline. Because these tasks do not have an alarming deadline, they can easily be ignored or postponed until the imminence of their completion date starts to threaten us.

When the pressure to complete these tasks starts to become heavy, they slip into the *'important-urgent'* category. When in this category, you can invest time in establishing good relations, averting problems, finding new opportunities, and planning for more important goals to be achieved in the future.

For over-delivering on your goals, the focus must be on things that are important and not just urgent. To avoid the stress of having too many critical deadlines, you must distinguish clearly between what is urgent and what is essential.

NOT URGENT-NOT IMPORTANT

These are essentially trivial activities that need to be ignored or delegated. On the contrary, what happens is that too often, we use our valuable time and energy on tasks that give us no return.

ABC OF SCHEDULING

Your daily schedule should reflect your long-term vision, purpose, and goals. To make sure that you create a vivid line of sight between your vision, purpose, and goals in your daily scheduling, I share a straightforward but unbelievably handy tool: The ABC of Scheduling.

'Must do' **A** Tasks: *(Do them great)*

You will start putting items on this list from your urgent-important category. You will also add important-not urgent tasks to it.

'Should do' **B** Tasks: *(Delegate them)*

This list can also include the same urgent-important and important-not urgent tasks. The only difference is that these tasks can always be effectively delegated to someone else.

'Do/Don't do' **C** Tasks: *(Put them last)*

These tasks include important-not urgent tasks for which there is no urgency, but you could spend some time doing them if you find the time.

CRITICAL & UNCRITICAL

If you are one of those who have *'too much to do'* and *think* they have *'too little time'* to do them, I have a solution. Start by breaking up your list into two categories: *critical* and *uncritical*.

Critical activities provide the most significant pay-off for our time; *'Uncritical'* activities give us emotional relief but do not advance our daily accomplishments very much. Accomplishing a *'critical'* thing means giving preference to *'business'* over *'busy-ness,'* favoring *'progress'* over *'wheel spinning.'*

When people open up their hearts, they disclose that they often spend a busy day at work, but when they get home at night, they know in their hearts that they have not accomplished anything. We may sometimes fool the world, but we cannot fool ourselves.

Doing critical things builds up our self-esteem and motivation level. Ever notice how, when you've had a productive *'critical'* day, the positive momentum carries forward into your evening hours?

Let's say it's the start of your workweek, and you have a lot of 'things to do,' some of which are 'critical,' others' uncritical.' When you begin your day, to what would you pay more attention to? The critical or uncritical tasks? You know what? When given a choice between 'critical' and 'uncritical' items, we almost always choose the 'uncritical' items and ignore the 'critical' items, even though we all want our day to be more productive.

Why? Because we are driven more by emotion than logic. You see, the 'critical' items are typically longer and harder to accomplish. The 'uncritical' items are typically quicker, more fun, and emotionally satisfying. If you are serious about improving your productivity, you need to cross over to the 'critical' side more often.

Excellent performance comes with the organization. Take a look at any top performer, and you will see clear evidence of self-organization surrounding his performance goals. Self-organization is almost a pre-requisite of over-delivering.

THREE QUICK SOLUTIONS

Whether you know it or not, your time bank has already received a fresh deposit of 168 hours at the beginning of the current week. No matter how you treated this capital so far, or what you do with the remaining supply stocked in the store, you *will* continue to get a regular supply of 168 hours *every week*, as long as you live.

With such a smooth and efficient supply chain, how come you complain about not having enough time? When does your time bank continue to refill automatically, how on earth can you grip on a *shortage* of time? If you are one of those who continuously grumble about a shortage of time, I have three quick solutions:

SLEEP A LITTLE LESS:

Do you know that we spend about a third of our week fast asleep? On ordinary people use up (I prefer to use the word 'waste') almost 50-70 hours sleeping every week. If you deduct, say, 60 hours from

168, you are left with only 108 hours a week to handle a variety of tasks and goals. So if you were to sleep a little less, you could automatically increase the number of hours available to you.

Some of you would find this extremely difficult, and you may have genuine reasons for this. Some people, though, use sleep merely as an excuse. Let me reassure you: Sleeping less will not harm you at all. Initially, you will probably face some discomfort, but with time, you will develop the habit of sleeping less. After all, God didn't send us into this world to *sleep*. We are here to accomplish some bigger goals.

CONTROL TIME THEFT:

It doesn't matter how many hours you sleep; my only suggestion is to stay *fully awake* during the remaining time.

Nobody can steal or rob your time if you are *fully* awake. Sleep time is dead time. During the time that you are not sleeping, you should come fully alive. You should demonstrate to the world that you are awake. And you should take full advantage of Tony Robbins' advice to 'awaken the giant within you.' When the giant within you is awake, you should look awake.

If you plan your day, define your priorities clearly, stick to your schedule, manage interruptions better and maintain a sense of focus, you could achieve a lot more in those 108 hours without compromising on your sleep time.

MAKE USE OF DELEGATION

'*Make use of delegation*,' I repeat.

'*But self-done is well done*,' you argue.

That is the most common argument used against delegation. We take great pride in doing things ourselves, don't we? *"If you want a job done right, you have to do it yourself,"* is one of the most frequently used clichés. It's careful thought, and it would make sense if we had an unlimited supply of time. Unfortunately, the truth is we don't.

If you still believe otherwise, you will be glad to know that you are wrong. And here is some bad news for you. If you insist on doing everything yourself, with *your hand*, you limit your ability to enhance your time.

You know why? Because you are relying on the limited time resources at your disposal, i.e., 108 hours only. The delegation, as I said earlier, allows you to benefit from other people's time. You tap into other people's time stream by getting them to do things for you. How does that feel? Would that multiply results for you?

When I say 'tap into others' time stream,' I don't mean *exploiting* people around you negatively or *using* them to achieve your wishes and hopes. I am proposing you use delegation as a tool for providing people around you an opportunity to realize their full potential.

LEVERAGE SUCCESS

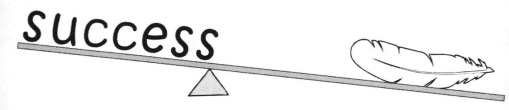

LEVERAGE SUCCESS

> *"The ability to influence a system, or an environment, in a way that multiplies the outcome of one's efforts without a corresponding increase in the consumption of resources. In other words, leverage is the advantageous condition of having a relatively small amount of cost yield a relatively high level of returns. See also financial leverage and operating leverage."*
>
> Source: http://www.businessdictionary.com

Have you ever stopped to think that in a horse race, the first horse across the finishing line may win a $10,000 prize and the second horse a mere $5,000?

Why does the first horse win *twice as much* money as the second horse? It's certainly not because it ran *twice as far* or *twice as fast*. It may have been 'just a *nose ahead*' of its nearest rival. I call this the *JANA Principle*.

JANA PRINCIPLE

Just
A
Nose
Ahead

What is the lesson to be learned here? You need not run *twice as fast* or put in *twice as much* effort to increase your daily success significantly. You only need to be a 'nose ahead' of where you already are. To be just a nose ahead, you will have to master the tools and strategies to leverage your success by creatively utilizing whatever you have.

Do not allow your mistakes and lapses to keep you from running at your full stretch and achieving the possible success. So never fail to get *a nose ahead* in all major areas of your life. You must fully leverage everything that you have, starting from your time, money, resources, talents, skills, attitude, opportunities, and possibilities.

Following are some straightforward laws, principles, strategies, and techniques that can help you actually *get a nose ahead.*

PEAK TIME

The metaphor of *peak time* can most easily be understood in the media context. Particularly on TV, if you wish to run a commercial during peak time, you have to pay a hefty amount of extra money. According to an NBC Survey Report:

An hour in Peak Time costs 900% higher than average hours.

You can use the same metaphor for leveraging your success. You will be surprised to know that *An hour in action in peak time is worth 4 hours of ordinary time.*

What is *Peak Time?*

It is the best time of your day. It is the time when your energy level is at its absolute peak. It is the time when anything and everything looks possible to you. Why is this so? Because your physical, neurological, and biological systems are supporting all your endeavors.

How can you leverage your success through peak time? By understanding and identifying *your energy curve.* If you pay close attention to your energy peaks and lows, you will find some useful hints. If you feel highly energetic, vibrant, and full of vitality during the early part of the day, then you are a morning person. That is your peak time. A few people achieve their peak of energy in the afternoon; others feel on top of the world in the evening. And then there are the night owls who can take up any creative challenge during the late-night hours because their creative force is at its optimum.

When you determine your peak performance time, your next *responsibility* should be to get the most from it. You can do three things to leverage your success by gaining the maximum benefit from your Peak Time:

1. Pursue your most vital goals during your peak time.
2. Avoid doing less essential things in peak times.
3. Do not struggle with difficult tasks when your energy levels are low.

PARETO PRINCIPLE

Pareto Principles is one of the best tools available on leveraging your success.

The Pareto Principle basically teaches us that 20% of our efforts produce 80% of our results. The additional 80% of our efforts will only yield an extra 20% of results. The first binge of effort, therefore, is the most productive use of our time. The latter thrust is very costly in terms of return on investment.

80 percent of your effectiveness is derived from 20 percent of your activities.

20% effort = 80% results

For example, let's say you allocate 2 hours (*which for the sake of argument represents 20% of your time*) to preparing for your upcoming report. You will be able to get it 80% right. It will not be perfect, but it will be accepted and appreciated by the client.

However, to squeeze out an additional 20% of results to make it a *'perfect report'* will require a further 80% of your time or 8 hours. Have you figured out that the additional results cost you sixteen times more in terms of effort than the initial results that you got from *20% of the exertion?*

The story does not end here. In your attempt to produce an additional 20% results, you miss out on the opportunity to leverage your success by focusing on accomplishing other *equally important* goals. After spending eight additional hours on the presentation, you will then probably complain, *'I didn't have time to accomplish other things. I am not a machine.'*

In all sincerity, you invested a reasonable amount of your time and prepared a pretty good report the first time around. It may not have been perfect, but putting in a lot more time to make it just *a little better* is not cost-effective and, therefore, not worth the extra effort.

I have personally known and worked with several individuals who suffer from what I call *perfection paralysis*. What they are pursuing is *perfection,* which practically speaking is unfeasible. For example, I cannot write a perfect article or a perfect book. I have been a victim of *perfection paralysis* for many years. Result? I could not produce anything.

Any book, article, report, or piece of writing can always be polished and improved upon with a little more time and effort. Still, if you focus on perfection (*with no focus on other equally essential priorities*), the only returns you will get are stress, frustration, and disappointment. Also, it will keep you away from leveraging your success.

If you still choose *perfection paralysis,* your overall productivity will suffer. Spending an excessive amount of time on a few things, trying to make them perfect (*at the cost of other crucial things*), is a sure-fail strategy. On the contrary, if you leverage the Pareto Principles and invest your energies in *essential* things, your productivity, success, and prosperity will be multiplied.

The other part of the principle is even more enjoyable. 80% additional effort produces ONLY 20% results.

80% EFFORT = 20% RESULTS

80% of your energy is usually spent on living areas, which yield just 20% of results; only 20% of your time is taken up by priorities that contribute to 80% of your achievement. *A small portion of your activities (20%) are vital, and they contribute the most toward your objectives.* A large portion of your activities (80%) are trivial in their contribution towards your objectives.

This suggests that many people, because they fail to leverage success, do not set priorities right and waste significant resources on minor, unimportant priorities. The key to higher productivity is separating the *vital* from the *trivial.* Once you understand this principle you should be immediately asking yourself three fundamental questions:

- What are my highest-value goals?
- What am I hired to *accomplish*?
- What should be the critical focus of my energy right now?

PERFECTION PARALYSIS

A small portion of your goals (20%), if leveraged well, can contribute the most in creating your best life. A large portion, however, is not leverage-able.

When I share this principle with participants during my sessions, many who have previously been unaware of it are shocked to realize the implications. The regional sales head of an FMCG company said to me in a tone of shock, 'That means only 20% of my customers give me 80% of my sales, and the other 80% account for merely 20% of my business? Now I know where I should have been spending 80% of my time. Thank you for bringing this to my notice. Now I will focus on the top 20% of my customers who bring 80% results.'

That is correct, I said. The Pareto Principle can leverage your success and save your life too. Apply it intelligently, carefully, and FULLY.

DELEGATION

'Leverage Success' requires a significant change in mindset. The traditional, regular thinking will not equip you to leverage opportunities for growth around you. One critical shift in thinking requires you to perceive the distinct difference between '*things you do'* and *'things you get done'*. You may not always find time for *'doing things,'* but you can *always* find time for *'getting things done'*.

Okay, let me ask you another question:

'How many hours in a day would you ideally like to have? More than 24 hours or less?'

Why do you always find that many people wish for a day comprised of more than 24 hours? Why do 24 hours seem to be insufficient to complete what people aspire to do?

How can we break the pattern of 'I *wish I had more time in a day, or I wish I had a 48-hour day'*?

'The only way to ensure that I will be able to get much more done is having at least a 48-hour day' is a very familiar excuse.

Unfortunately, because of cosmic reasons, a 48-hour day is impossible. We can't get more than 24 hours out of each day. But the good news is that if you sacrifice your sleep for any given number of hours, you can start receiving a new supply of hours each day, starting from today. Sound interesting?

You do not care much for the idea? Okay, I have another one. One better piece of news is that you can actually leverage the time available to you by tapping into other people's *time stream*.

How do we tap into others' time stream? By delegation, of course! By plugging into someone else's time stream (when we don't have the time or the expertise), we can multiply our results without demanding additional hours.

"Delegation is your ability to plug into someone else's time river due to lack of time or expertise to leverage success and multiply the results"

EFFECTIVE DELEGATION:

Delegation becomes essential when you don't have the time or the expertise to do something. That offers the opportunity to delegate, thereby leveraging success for yourself and for the whole organization.

Imagine for a moment that all of us had to do *everything* ourselves, washing clothes, cooking food, building homes, cleaning bathrooms, weeding gardens, milking cows, mopping floors, stitching clothes, etc. How would it feel? I believe the average person would probably lose 95% of what they have now or retain a mere 5% of what they have achieved.

So what is the point I am making here? The point is that you are already convinced about the *idea* of delegation and are employing it in some areas of your life. Taking it a step forward, you need to decide '*how far you want to go with it*'. If you decide to delegate wisely and appropriately, the delegation will open up the door to leverage greater success. You will no longer be at the mercy of those 108 hours every week.

The delegation, if appropriately used, can incredibly facilitate your growth and development, including:

- Getting more time to concentrate on priority work
- Making use of other people's exceptional skills
- Doing things faster through concurrent activity
- Creating future resources to handle similar tasks and goals

BENEFITS OF DELEGATION

When you consider delegation, don't merely focus on the benefits *you* get. You can bring into play the '*purpose*' philosophy. Delegation is not merely about *getting*, it's primarily about *giving*. The person being *delegated to* also benefits if you delegate intending to help others grow. The benefits you can provide others include:

- Recognizing their importance
- Giving them a chance to use and sharpen their special skills
- Giving people much-needed attention
- Creating opportunities for people to get additional rewards and incentives
- Building self-confidence of your team
- Providing opportunities to learn and grow
- Facilitating the process of skill-building

PSYCHOLOGICAL BARRIERS:

A vast majority of managers do not use delegation, even though delegation brings lots of benefits to the *delegator* and *delegatee*. As a psychologist, I have reached the conclusion that people avoid delegating because of some psychological hang-ups. Our research reveals three significant psychological barriers to delegation:

1. **Fear of surrendering authority:**

That is the biggest block. *'I might lose my authority over people.'*

2. **Fear of mistakes:**

'Others will commit errors, and I will have to re-do it. An advanced form of this barrier is *'What if I make a mistake while delegating, what if I delegate to the wrong person and that person doesn't deliver on time?'*

3. **Fear of invisibility:**

Visibility sometimes becomes more important than ability. *'The top management will think I am doing nothing.'*

EXCUSES FOR NOT DELEGATING

A few people succeed in overcoming the psychological barriers, but they still cannot delegate because they have protected themselves by inventing particular excuses for not delegating. Our research discloses a list of critical excuses people use for not delegating hence not being able to leverage success. You can also see my response to these excuses:

1. I know I can do it better.
   You have enough time to do all the essential things yourself?

2. It's my job
   That's why it needs to be done. What is the surest way of getting it done?

3. I am insecure
   Because you do not trust the abilities of the people around you. When their resource pool becomes yours, you will feel more confident and secure.

4. I am not clear about my own role.
   Performing an analysis of what can be delegated to others will automatically bring clarity to your own role.

5. Others already have enough to do
   That's a real good one. And don't you already have a lot to do? Think about creating an opportunity to delegate.

6. I am unable or unwilling.
   Please let go!!!

7. Lack of faith in subordinates' abilities
   Have faith in your people. Only they can help you rise.

8. I am afraid that my subordinates will perform better than me.
   Great news! What more could a manager want? Get rid of your fears.

9. I believe I can do it quicker and better myself.
   That's right. And hold on to that belief that no one else can do the most daunting, alarming, and threatening tasks.

10. I like to give the impression of being overworked.
    You will give a far better impression if you actually accomplish things and show results to the top management.

11. I enjoy doing the job.
    Maybe someone else will find it equally enjoyable.

12. I have no time to work out what the job entails.
    The delegation will allow you the time to work it out.

DON'T DELEGATE

I do not suggest you delegate everything, as the delegation is not a solution to every management problem. You cannot and should not use delegation in every situation. Some areas or situations where you should not even consider delegating are:

- Planning key projects
- Selecting a team for a project
- Motivating team members
- Monitoring team efforts
- Evaluating team members
- Rewarding team members

When delegating, you must delegate to the right person, delegate the right task, and ensure clear communication.

DELEGATION PROCESS

Delegation does not automatically produce results. You will have to keep a sharp eye on the overall delegation process. The key steps involved in the effective delegation include the following:

1. **Objectives:**

   What are the key results you would like to achieve through this task? What is the final outcome you are aiming at?

2. **Deadline:**

   The final deadline for completing the task should be clearly communicated, understood, and agreed upon.

3. **Ownership:**

   Who is eventually responsible for the completion of this task? Who is the real owner?

4. **Support:**

   What information, resources, and help will the other person require from you to produce the desired results?

5. **Monitoring:**

   How would you ensure effective monitoring of the task? What methods of supervision will you choose?

6. **Evaluation:**

   How will you evaluate the goal? What is the criteria to be used to evaluate the success of the task? Have you shared this criteria with the person to whom you are delegating?

7. **Feedback:**

What will be the medium for sharing feedback?

- How often will you give your feedback?
- What impact will this feedback have on your future relations with this person?
- Will this feedback help you and any other persons handle delegation more effectively in the future?

REVERSE DELEGATION

Are you aware of the concept of '*Reverse Delegation*'?

Reverse delegation is a widespread phenomenon. You delegate something to someone, and the other person comes back to you time and again for assistance or advice, to the extent that you end up virtually doing the task yourself. Instead of holding the person responsible for completing the task, the other person regularly monitors your progress on the task you initially assigned to him.

ACTIONS:

1. Examine your reasons for resisting delegation
2. Delegate to keep people involved
3. Delegate recurring tasks
4. Define the job and results carefully
5. Resist the temptation to interfere unnecessarily with the *delegatee*

Provide opportunities to people around you, and they will go the extra mile to rise to your level of expectation. Lift them up, place them on a higher pedestal through intelligent use of delegation. Remember, that's how you grew and got to your present level.

Use delegation as an instrument to create a victory for the person being delegated to as well. Delegation is not dumping. It is an excellent way of bringing out the best in people and leverage success for everyone.

LIVE 100%

LIVE 100%

> *"Leaders who can stay optimistic and upbeat, even under intense pressure, radiate the positive feelings that create resonance. By staying in control of their feelings and impulses, they craft an environment of trust, comforts, and fairness. And that self-management has a trickle-down effect from the leader."*
> — *Daniel Goleman, Primal Leadership*

Live 100% means living life at its fullest. And what does it involve? Different people will have different definitions of what an abounding life is. Living life at 100% would imply being grateful for what you have and making a commitment to continue your journey to what you wish to achieve. Living 100% means living with an attitude of gratitude and having a sense of inner fulfillment.

Ask yourself, what does living 100% require? My research has revealed a variety of responses to this question: freedom, resources, and ability to have fun, a sense of purpose, sensitivity to pain, a readiness for enjoyment, being fully involved in life, etc.

You will probably have noticed that minimal needs to come from the outside to live life at its fullest.

LIVING 100% MEANS

1. Living consciously, not sleepwalking
2. Being able to realize your full potential
3. Believing in yourself, challenging and breaking limits
4. Going beyond your fears
5. Serving the world, not just yourself
6. Cultivating supportive relations
7. Leaving a legacy that society is proud of

ACHIEVEMENT & FULFILLMENT

There are two kinds of human beings on this planet:

TYPE 01:

Highly successful people with plenty of achievements on their credit. The world knows them as high achievers. They have medals, trophies, certificates, titles, accolades, prizes, honors, and awards. However, they still feel a sense of void in their life. This dissatisfaction stems from two things.

One, they have compromised their fundamental values and principles to achieve this success. The sense of achievement has cost them too much. They indeed have paid a heavy price for being here. They now believe that they put too much value on things they don't value anymore.

Two, this achievement has nothing to do with their sense of purpose and passion. People remained alien to the concept of direction. Even if they found some purpose, they could never align it with their most genuine potential.

TYPE 02:

People in category #2 stand no chance to be considered as high achievers. They probably have nothing on their credit to show. However, these people feel a fantastic sense of fulfillment deep inside them. They don't fulfill the success criteria i.e., cars, status, titles, positions, awards, etc. but they inevitably experience an inner delight.

If you are in any of the above two categories, I have bad news for you. You have lived life, only 50%. Aiming to experience either achievement or fulfillment is not doing justice to your existence. This relationship is not based on *or*, it is based on *and*.

Living 100% means living life so that you experience both achievement and fulfillment at the most appropriate time of your life.

There is nothing wrong with having those cars, overflowing bank accounts, penthouses, jets, beach huts, personalized islands, and lush lifestyles. It's only wrong if the path leading you here has witnessed compromises on principles, values, integrity, and personal honor. Also, it will be less fulfilling if your passion and purpose have not accompanied you on this journey.

THE MOMENT OF YOUR LIFE

Your most reasonable excuses for not living life at its fullest could be 'Freedom comes with success and prosperity' or 'I don't have the material resources'. I can tell you with great certainty that the joy of living is not reliant on owning money or other material resources.

In a study, we asked people to express the best moments of their lives. We wanted to find out what they considered their life's peak. Care to see the answers?

- Falling in love
- Laughing till your stomach hurts
- Enjoying a drive in the countryside
- Listening to your favorite song on the radio
- Falling asleep listening to the rain drumming down outside
- Getting out of the shower and wrapping yourself in a warm towel
- Passing your final exams with good grades
- Being part of an exciting conversation
- Finding some money in the pocket of an old pair of trousers
- Laughing at yourself
- Sharing an ordinary meal with your friends
- Laughing without a reason
- *'Accidentally'* hearing someone say something beautiful about you
- Watching the sunset
- Listening to a song that reminds you of an essential person in your life
- Receiving or giving your first ... ...
- Feeling a lift in your heart when seeing your *'special'* someone
- Having a great time with your family
- Seeing the one, you love
- Wearing the shirt of a person you love and smelling his/her fragrance
- Being reunited with a family member after a long time
- Reading or listening to poetry

Did the list touch your heart? Did it change your thinking about living life at its fullest?

Do you still believe you need money or other financial resources to enjoy life's most cherished moments? Believe it or not, life's best gifts are free. But we have no time to enjoy them.

To enjoy living life at its peak, you just need to involve yourself fully in living. Don't sleepwalk. Don't let those beautiful moments go without celebrations. Don't let life and its joy pass you by. Freeze them, capture them, embrace them, and clasp them tightly to you until you squeeze the most from each precious moment of your life.

LIVING 100% EVERY DAY

Living 100% will take place one day at a time. So let's focus on making that one day the best day of your life. I am going to share fundamental steps to help you set the foundation for living each day to its fullest.

1. QUALITY SLEEP

High-quality sleep refreshes you and gives you a heightened sense of vitality and energy. Sleep provides a feeling of reinvigoration and rejuvenation. But you don't need to sleep longer to get that feeling. You can actually manage your sleep time the way you want.

2. POWER START

Jump out of bed in the morning. Why? Because a part of you says '*get up,*' and the other part tempts you to '*sleep just a little more*'. And you know which part usually wins. Drink a full glass of water as soon as you wake up. During sleep, your body becomes quite dehydrated, causing you to feel fatigued. Drinking water guarantees instant energy.

Do full stretches with your arms, legs, neck; this increases the circulation of the blood to various parts of your body. Start your day thinking about that one overriding desire. This desire should be impressive, so mind-blowing that it supersedes every negative or non-productive thought that may cross your mind in the morning.

3. MORNING QUESTIONS

I learned this concept from my coach Tony Robbins. In his book 'Awaken the Giant Within', he shared a list of morning questions you can ask yourself to develop a sharp focus on the positive elements of life. These questions include:

- *What am I happy about?*
- *What am I grateful for?*
- *What is working for me?*
- *Why am I blessed?*
- *What gifts has God given me?*

4. MOTION CREATES EMOTION

To ensure that you will have a high-energy day, use body movement to generate energy. Energy is not generated by lying down on a bed or relaxing in a chair. An abrupt change in your tone of voice and body movement creates an instant rush of vibrancy.

5. BALANCED BREAKFAST

Skipping breakfast is no act of bravery. I cannot overemphasize enough the importance of having the most essential meal of your day – *breakfast.*

6. MOTIVATIONAL TAPES/MUSIC

Turn your car into an *automobile university.* I learned this unique concept from my coach Brian Tracy. Switch on your cassette player and listen to motivational and educational tapes in your car. It will elevate your mood and frame of mind, but it will also hone your skills.

7. TAKING A LUNCH BREAK

While over-extending yourself is not recommended, never have lunch *alone*. Use this time to interact with a co-worker, client, or prospect.

8. EXERCISE AT YOUR DESK:

Taking a small break for exercise re-energizes you. You can spare a few seconds to do a little exercise at your desk. Stop work for 30 seconds and do something that guarantees fun.

9. QUEST OF ALIGNMENT:

The whole day should be focused on the living on purpose, unleashing your passion, and doing your very best in whatever you do. When your purpose, passion, and performance are aligned, living 100% is guaranteed.

Living 100% is a purposeful decision and a deliberate choice. When you choose to look for opportunities, you will find them in abundance and enjoy them for sure. Living life at its fullest means, you will refuse to sit in the passenger seat. Instead, you will take the driving seat in your life. From being a spectator, you jump into the stadium and take a full part in the game of life.

LIVING A GORGEOUS LIFE

Living 100% is like walking a tightrope. On that tightrope, you do not just walk; you try to balance the various elements of your life:

family, work, health, and finances. Remember the broken table leg metaphor in the first principle of this book? If one leg is uneven, the entire balance goes off. You are at risk of falling. Right?

Living 100% is about maintaining a perfect balance (not an easy task) between the four fundamental elements of your life. Not being able to pay adequate attention to these elements will create a severe imbalance, causing a major crisis in your life.

The core of Living 100% is *'balance'*. When you neglect family, hoping all will be okay, you meet bad surprises. 'What is the best place to take your four-year-old daughter on vacation?'

My answer is: *'You take her when she's four years old.'*

> Research reveals that the average working person spends less than two minutes per day in meaningful communication with their spouse or 'significant others' and less than thirty seconds per day in meaningful communication with their children.

Living 100% is not possible without your physical well-being. You don't have time for quality sleep, and on top of it, you eat food that is unsafe, unhealthy, and risky. It has been years since you took any exercise or fitness classes. Do you know that 90% of those who join health and fitness clubs today will stop going within the next 90 days? You may be surprised to learn that many people spend more time taking care of their new cars than on taking care of themselves. For a change, how about taking yourself in for scheduled maintenance, putting the right rated fuel in your emotional energy tank, and keeping your heart, mind, and body shiny and squeaky clean?

By now, I believe you have become pretty sensitive and committed to taking care of your family and your own health. How about securing a balance in your financial life? Is financial freedom one of your key goals in life? Do you spend time daily to accomplish this goal?

Have you seen people who spend a lot of time with family and look at the picture of health, but have no money to support the expenses of their daily lives? Would your family still be happy if they had no financial security?

Living 100% requires ensuring the right investment focus in building and expanding your financial security. My coach, Jim Rohn, once asked me, 'How much money have you saved and invested in the last five years?' His question came as a big shock to me. I lived my life with a carefree philosophy of 'borrow today and (try to) return tomorrow'. Once I developed a sensitivity to this question, I was able to achieve financial freedom. How much money have you saved and invested in the last five years?

Would you relish the financial freedom, if you feel you didn't enjoy the work that got you this money?

What meaning does work have in your life? Do you work because you have to or because you want to? Ninety-seven percent of people in a survey responded that they would not continue with their current employer or current work line if they achieved financial freedom.

Would you still continue in your current job if you did not have to make a deliberate effort to earn money? What would motivate you then if earning money were not on your agenda list? Are constant education and learning among your priorities in life? Wouldn't you like to be known as an expert in your field, someone you look up to for guidance, advice, and professional support? Are you one of those who do not care to invest in their own professional development, who buy books but do not read them?

Do you update your professional knowledge regularly? Are you coping with the ever-changing demands of your job? Are you taking advantage of the opportunities for advancement available in your field of expertise? Are you satisfied with your 'play it safe' policy?

Many people remain so busy in their so-called routine lifestyle that they do not network with the right people. You must build a web of essential relationships around you to climb the ladder of success more rapidly.

Living 100% would be half-finished even if you achieve a good sense of balance between your family, health, finance, and work but have no connection with the creator. Without a spiritual bond with a higher power, life seems to lack meaning or purpose.

FOUR LAWS OF LIVING 100%

Did you know '*forgetting*' can play a vital role in helping you live to the fullest?

Forgetting is a gift. Especially when forgetting the boundaries that you think define you. Forgetting is a blessing when you forget the limits that hold you back. Forgetting is a gift when you forget your fears, apprehensions, worries, and negativities.

What does your FORGET CATALOGUE tell you?

Take only 10 minutes to make a list of all the things you would like to forget. Start making that list now. Don't delay. Kickstart now! This is your life. Only you can live it. So why living on 50% of it. The remaining 50% is absolute of no use to anyone. No need to sacrifice your way of living 100%. Do whatever it takes to make you feel deep inside that you live 100%—every moment to its fullest. Start living your 100% now.

Together, let's make a commitment today to forget all those obstacles on our way to success.

When I did this exercise,

Forget HESITATION, because it will never let you take the giant leap toward a purposeful life.

Forget HOPELESSNESS, because losing hope indeed is a sin. Use the conviction 'I will prevail in the end' to rejuvenate you.

Forget HELPLESSNESS, because your creator has given you the power to change any element of your life.

Forget POWERLESSNESS, because you have all the power within. You may have no idea, but the power to turn nothing into something is within you.

FLAG OF LIFE

Have you ever seen a flag carrying on it the slogan to Live 100%? If you wish to live life at its peak, holding that flag up will be a pre-requisite. Seeing this flag in your hand, others will recognize you even from a distance. They will know you are the one who has mastered the art of top living. What is this flag? What does this flag represent?

The FLAG signifies the four core emotions of your life. Living 100% is impossible without experiencing these four emotions. Only those who ride the full swing of these four feelings can understand what living 100% really means.

1. FORGIVE

Forgiveness is a prime emotion. It is the surest path to fulfillment. What is the opposite of forgiving? Revenge? Anger? Fury?

Resentment? Wrath? Anguish? And how do you feel when your heart is filled with anger, hate, and revenge?

Try forgiveness. Don't allow negative emotions to dwell in your heart. Kick them out. Practice forgiveness.

2. LOVE

Love is one of the two most powerful emotions any human being can ever experience. The other is 'fear'. I wish you fill your heart with love.

3. APOLOGIZE

Seeking an apology for your mistakes doesn't put you down. It doesn't belittle you. When you make a sincere apology, even the most hardened hearts will meltdown.

4. GRATITUDE

Gratitude is at the core of peak living. Without gratitude, you don't even deserve the right to use the word 'living at 100%'. Living with an attitude is gratitude is the decisive key to success.

AMPLIFY EXECUTION

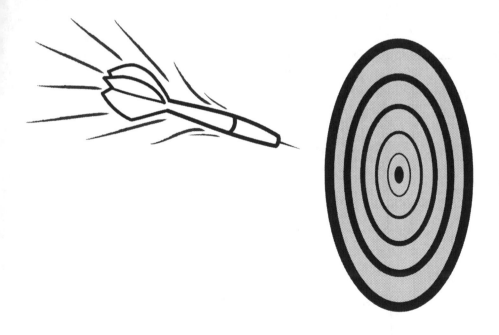

AMPLIFY EXECUTION

Have you seen people who do more in a month than others can manage in a year? Examples abound all around us. I have a friend, Arif Anees, who can accomplish in a day what would take his colleagues at least a week to do. And I am not exaggerating. He is a veritable giant when it comes to performance.

What is the secret of people like Arif Anees? What gives them the ability to accomplish what they accomplish? Would you be interested in discovering their secret?

I once asked Arif the same question. He leaned towards me and whispered in my ear in a confiding tone, '*The truth is I possess some magic!*'

What? Magic?

I have a magic wand that expands my day.

Magic wand? Where on earth did you get it?

This magic wand has the name 'execution'.

My face must have betrayed my disappointment.

'Disappointed?' Arif smiled. 'I knew you would be. We all have the same twenty-four hours in a day, so what kind of magic lets me expand my twenty-four hours? The answer is putting every idea, thought or plan into execution.'

We all want to get richer *quicker.* We want everything *now.* We want fast promotions, quick sales, speedy growth, immediate profits, swift accomplishment, and rapid returns on our investments. This chapter is about getting results and getting them faster. Apart from spurring your inner drive for success, it also facilitates you in developing the momentum to make things happen sooner. You are going to learn to create results within months, which will take others' years to achieve.

07 EXECUTION KILLERS

Wanting something is not enough. You must hunger for it. Your motivation must be compelling to overcome the obstacles that will invariably come your way.
Les Brown

1. **Indecision:**

   You worry about the Excuses without ever taking any decision to deal with them.

2. **Inefficiency:**

   Jumping into action without first analyzing the impact or outcomes of your actions

3. **Inaction:**

   Passively waiting for things to happen on their own. Failing to get things done at the right time

4. **Tunnel thinking:**

    Not willing to see what is coming ahead. No attention is given to planning and a lack of contingency plans

5. **Unnecessary errors:**

    Claiming not to have enough time to do things right but later having all the time to do it over

6. **Crisis:**

    Focusing on urgent rather than essential tasks, turning them into a crisis

7. **Poor organization:**

    Poorly managed work station, office, filing system and papers

EXECUTION FILTERS

You are not supposed to go for mindless execution. Before you decided to invest your energy in executing something, you got to make sure that this is something worthy of execution.

Amplifying execution doesn't mean executing the wrong stuff. You will only bring something from the start to the finish line if it passes the 5-D Test.

8. **DROP IT**

    What will happen if you don't accomplish this at all? Are you ready to face the consequences of not doing it? The fundamental principle behind this tool is 'Never manage what you can eliminate.'

9. DELEGATE IT

Do you have someone who can take care of this task? Can it be delegated in a way that ensures the same results? Do you have someone ready to whom you can delegate it?

10. DELAY IT

If you cannot drop a task or find anyone to whom you can delegate it, the delay is the next logical choice. But keep in mind that this is not a delay in the negative sense. It is accepting the reality that you don't have enough time right now due to your commitment to some real high-priority tasks.

11. DISSECT!

Even if the delay is not possible, and you are pressed with equally essential priorities, here is another solution. Slice up the goals into many chunks. You may not have the time to execute the whole plan, but you can finish off one chunk.

12. DELIGHT IN IT!

'It can't be delayed' is the answer. If that's the case, then you are left with only one option: *Delight in it*. Why? Because now you *have* to do it and turning a 'have to do it' into a 'want to do it' is the difference between doing it under stress and executing it without joy.

POWER OF EFFECTENCY

If you are ready, here goes another tool: *effectency*. I hope that by now, you have clearly understood the difference between efficient execution and effective execution. Just to clarify it one more time, *efficient* execution focuses on doing things faster. Thus, finding a way to complete a task more rapidly reflects *efficiency*.

A practical execution approach, on the other hand, ensures the achievement of the *right* outcome. To summarize, efficiency is about *executing things right*, while effectiveness is about *'executing the right things'*.

Over the last many years, I am promoting a *new* approach that combines efficiency and effectiveness. I prefer to call it *'effectency'*; that means choosing the *'right'* things to do and then finding the most efficient way of doing them. If you pay close attention, you will realize that *effectency* is a mindset that is fundamental to execution and accelerating results in life. You certainly do not want to create the wrong results faster!

> *'Every significant change comes from within.'*
> *Dr. Alan Baugh, Author of 'Wake-Up Calls'*

PARKINSON'S LAW

> *"To finish work? To finish a picture? What nonsense! To finish it means to be through with it, kill it, rid it of its soul, and give it its final blow the coup de grace for the painter and the picture."*
> *Pablo Picasso*

Are you ready to get another handy execution tool?

Parkinson's Law says, "Work expands to fill the time available for its completion."

Interesting? Let me put it to you another way: What this Law means is, *'We always take as much time as we are given to do a job.'*

You might have noticed that a project tends to expand with the time **you** assign to it. If you set yourself one goal to accomplish, it will take you all day. If you set yourself two goals, you will get them both done. If you aim for twelve tasks to complete, you may not get all twelve done, but you will probably get eight or nine. Having a lot to do creates a healthy sense of pressure on us to get things done.

How can the application of Parkinson's Law upscale your execution rate? You may not like my answer; you have overloaded your day!

Prepare a daily action plan that includes not only the things you '*have to do,*' but the things you '*want to do.*' With the positive pressure, you almost automatically execute better. You are less likely to suffer interruptions.

Remember: 'If you want to get something done, give it to a busy person.'

Another way of benefiting from this principle is to ask yourself this simple question: *What if I had only half the time to complete the job?*

List some routine tasks that you can do in half the time? That includes both personal and professional tasks. List the chores along with the amount of time they take. You can also estimate the amount of time you could save on each task by applying Parkinson's Law. This additional supply of time can be utilized for doing the things you never get time to do.

Applying Parkinson's Law has saved me several hundred hours in the last fourteen years. You just need to break away from your ingrained thinking about taking a set number of hours to execute specific tasks. This one mindset shift will amplify your execution and provide you free space to take on additional challenges head-on.

LAW OF INCREASING RETURNS

The Law of Increasing Returns states, 'The better you get at doing something, the lesser amount of time it takes to get done.'

On the face of it, such a simple law, but so extremely difficult to put into practice. Why would such a simple law be so challenging to apply? Because the keywords in this Law are *getting better*'. The reverse of this Law is also true: 'If you don't get better at doing something, you will keep taking the same amount of time (or more) to get it done.'

If you want to *amplify execution* and accelerate your results, the best way is to expand your competence, work harder on your personality, improve your skills, and learn ways to do your work better. If you don't hone your skills, you will remain where you are.

When you challenge yourself to improve your performance a little more each time, your skill level inevitably increases. Not only does the quality of your results improve, but the amount of time it takes to complete it is significantly reduced.

What possible application can the Law of Increasing Returns have in your life? Take two straightforward steps to benefit from this Law:

STEP 01:

Identify those few *key result areas* in your professional life that make a significant contribution to your career growth. Your promotion, growth, increment, and success are largely dependent on your performance in these *vital result* indicators.

STEP 02:

Simply become excellent at performing in these *key result areas.* Raise the bar, expect more from yourself, challenge your performance, set some challenging performance goals, and surprise yourself with your performance. Aim to ensure that there is no one better than you in these critical areas.

Trust me, the time, energy, and focus you invest in achieving excellence in these *key* result areas will give you an unbelievably high return.

SWITCH TIME

This is one of the most amazing concepts in amplifying execution. When I was introduced to this concept, it accelerated my results to an incredible extent.

The simplest definition of Switch Time is 'the odd pieces of time between everything you do'.

Now you need to spot all those *'betweens'* in your day. Switch Time is the time between two essential activities, especially when you are waiting for people or waiting for something to happen.

The time you spend waiting at a doctor's reception room, commuting, driving, standing in line, or waiting for something can be defined as Switch Time. I call it *wasted time* as it comes so suddenly and unexpectedly that it goes unutilized. Therefore it does not bring about any results for you.

When I struggled to make a career, I had problems finding enough time to do the things that could accelerate my growth. I had a distinct idea of what those things were but could not find the time to hone my skills in those areas. I realized that enhancing my reading, writing, and public speaking skills, in particular, could speed up my results in life.

I spent almost all day on the road, visiting places, appearing for interviews, and showing up for appointments. I also realized that a lot of my time was wasted merely sitting idle in reception rooms, waiting in line at the bus stop, traveling on vans, and walking in the street (I could barely afford public transport).

Once I realized how much time was being wasted, I made a plan to give life to my dead time. I started carrying a 'switch folder' with me to include articles, books, and some other reading and writing material.

I became so obsessed with the idea that I started utilizing every minute. Whether it was a noisy bus stop, a reception area, or a crowded public bus, I could utilize the time to both *read* and *write*. Initially, it was tough to concentrate, but I soon developed the mindset and the ability to focus on what I wanted to achieve, and not let any distraction stop me from achieving it.

My coach Jim Rohn suggested I listen to personal development audio cassettes in my car. Of course, it never occurred to him that I did not possess a car. But the day I got my first car, I converted it into a learning machine and started listening to his cassettes in the car. I found that turning my automobile into a mobile classroom was an enriching experience.

My habit of making use of every available moment still helps me. After developing the ability to read while standing on a public bus, or hovering on the rooftop of a bus, anything less uncomfortable is a piece of cake. I did not miss the opportunity to develop myself through reading even if I happen to be in a *'Qingqi rickshaw'* sitting behind the driver with another passenger seated behind me. I prop my book between the driver and myself and start reading, no matter how bone-rattling the ride turns out to be.

Do you recall the definition of Switch Time?

'The odd pieces of time between everything you do'

These odd pieces together amount to a cumulative loss of many hours at the end of the day. As these are *unexpected* odd pieces, you tend to leave them fallow without sowing any self-development.

The UILI Formula can help you make better decisions about those *odd pieces of time between everything you do.* UILI stands for:

USE IT OR LOSE IT

And remember, don't become too obsessed with calculations about the time lost between activities. The objective here is to amplify execution by getting the most from time while not becoming a work machine. You can also use *Switch Time* for relaxation, deep breathing, beautiful moments of your life, reading poetry, praying silently, and developing a connection with your creator.

The point I am making here is that this time should not go to waste *unnoticed and unrealized.* Developing sensitivity to this issue will help you amplify execution in your life without stressing yourself.

POWER TOOLS FOR AMPLIFY EXECUTION

WAWA RULE

WAWA stands for:

What
Actually
Was
Accomplished

The goal here is to ensure that something of significance is accomplished.

MULTI-TASKING:

Another handy tool to accelerate results is multi-tasking. It is accessible to every one of us. Multi-tasking means doing several things at the same time.

You may learn this lesson from homemakers. They cook food, wash dishes and clothes, attend to their kids, all at the same time. We all do multi-tasking in our offices all day. But whenever you decide to do more than one thing at the same time, you have to be very careful in choosing the activities. (For instance, don't attempt multi-tasking when your spouse is saying something to you!) The risk with multi-tasking is that you can mess up all your activities and produce zero results for all the tasks.

START AND END TIMES

A very effective strategy to accomplish and execute more is to decide in advance the start and finish times for each activity. Not deciding an end time means you are leaving the door open for the activity just to drag on.

ALLOTMENT

Keeping the nature of your work in view, you can choose specific days for certain activities. For instance, whatever you wish to accomplish during a given week, you could decide on a specific day for each particular task or activity. If your job is predictable and you know your routine well, you could also allocate a few tasks only on specific days.

Allocating certain days to specific tasks allows you to focus on a few, but significantly important, things.

CUT OFF

High achievers amplify execution by cutting themselves off from all distractions and activities that impede their progress, such as phones, voice mail, text messages, email, social media, etc.

This is a beneficial technique. After allocating a certain period to a specific goal, you disconnect yourself entirely from every other activity. This act of disassociation does not abruptly take place.

Proper planning allows you the room to disassociate yourself so that you can focus on one task while other tasks are also being taken care of. Naturally, you cannot just vanish from the scene to take care of one matter, leaving the rest of your responsibilities unattended.

STAY VIBRANT

To accelerate results, it is necessary to maintain a stable energy level throughout the day. Instead of coffee in the afternoon, try a small, sugar-free snack instead.

While caffeine and sugar can give your energy a slight boost when it is flagging, they can result in an energy crash after the effects subside. Drink lots of water and fresh juices to keep yourself vibrant, energetic, and animated.

GET THE MOST FROM YOUR DAY

You can take some simple steps to get the most from your day:

1. Break down your daily tasks further to fit into the blocked time.
2. When aiming to complete several tasks within a short period, never forget to maintain quality in the most important.
3. Make sure you are doing tasks that are aligned with your values, beliefs, and rules.
4. It is okay to make mistakes, but it is *not* okay to repeat the same mistake repeatedly.
5. Handle one thing at a time, because when your focus on the task in hand is not 100%, you end up cheating yourself and not utilizing your energy to its fullest.

EARN YOUR ROTI

Without having a clear sense of priorities, plans remain just plans. While prioritizing, use a simple principle: Earn your ROTI. That stands for

Return
On
Time
Invested

Whether a task becomes a priority or not depends on the return, it can offer on the amount of time invested. The higher the expectation of return, the higher the task should be positioned in the *to-do* list.

I was somewhat puzzled when I first read the phrase '*If you need something done, give it to a busy person*'. But later on, I found this to be extremely apt. Why? Because busy people don't have any time to waste. And they also know the value of their time.

When you have a full schedule, you will not have time to waste on being unproductive. Time wasters will begin to realize that they will have to schedule time with you if they intend to try wasting your time.

10 WAYS OF AMPLIFY EXECUTION

You can find below ten ways to accomplish more in less time:

1. Wake up early
2. Make a mental sketch for your day *and put it on paper*
3. Eat a good breakfast
4. Overload your day
5. Prepare a goal scrapbook and put your goals into writing
6. Work with a clean desk
7. Listen to educational tapes in your car
8. Plan and take vacations
9. Don't believe in 'Someday I'll...'
10. Do a nightly 30-second review

RE-INVENT DAILY

RE-INVENT DAILY

*People who cannot invent and re-invent themselves must be content with
borrowed postures, secondhand ideas, fitting in instead of standing out.*
Warren Bennis

Once upon a time, there was a wave. A little wave. Bobbling along in
the ocean. Having a wonderful time. She was enjoying the wind and
the fresh air. Suddenly she got saddened to see the other waves in front
of her, crashing against the shore.

'My God, this terrible,' the wave says. 'Look what's going to happen
to me!'

Then along comes another wave. It sees the first wave, looking
grim, and it says to her, 'Why do you look so sad?'

The first wave replies, 'You don't understand, we're all going to crash!
All of us waves are going to be nothing! Isn't it terrible?'

The second wave says: 'No, you don't understand. You're not a wave,
you're part of the ocean.'

Source: "Tuesdays With Morrie" by Mitch Albom

Like the little wave, all of us are challenged to re-invent who we are at some point in life. What are we doing? Why are we here? What bigger picture we are part of? Who is with us in this picture? How can we rejuvenate a sense of belongingness with our environment?

How can we generate energy from the adversity? How can we reframe the meaning of draining events taking place around us? How can we reignite a sense of purpose? What changes in our thinking, feeling, and behavior we need to instill to keep moving forward?

None of these questions is easy to answer. It is easy, however, to skip the questions. By skipping, you choose to remain stuck in the old patterns of thinking and behaving. Taking you nowhere.

Re-inventing begins with a decision to open your heart and mind to the changing realities of the world. Your openness to re-invent yourself shows you are flexible, ready to change, open to feedback, and prepared to handle uncertainty, risk, and ambiguity.

RE-INVENTING IS NOT OPTIONAL

Success doesn't mean being an ultra-rich, super-efficient, unapproachable work machine. The idea is for you to lead a life hallmarked by satisfaction, prosperity, and fulfillment.

Living your purpose and passion for optimizing performance is the ultimate way of life. To stay on this path, you will be required to constantly 're-invent' yourself. You know why? Because, if you didn't do anything new to yourself, you would remain the same.

Re-inventing is not once in a lifetime activity. The world around you is changing so fast. Trailing your purposeful life while releasing your true potential is rarely a smooth quest. To grow continually, you will have to outpace the change. You don't have to remain today who you were when you began this chase. To secure victory, you have to consistently outgrow your limits, hurdles, and blockades.

In this hunt so far, even if you have failed more than what you expected. It's acceptable. If you found yourself weaker than you could imagine, it is still reasonable. If you choose to learn from your own journey, you will *know* that the rough experiences you sailed through, the hard-hitting disappointment you embraced, the bumpy roads that ran you in circles, and the spiky obstacles you survived; have taken you to a higher level of awareness. All of it has conspired to make you wiser, more intelligent, and sensible.

BENEFITS

Time, effort, and resources invested in 're-inventing' yourself will guarantee a big payoff. The return on investment is enormous. The renewed sense of re-inventing brings the following benefits to you:

- You either re-assure your finding or re-discover from scratch, who you are?
- You dig new wells to constantly re-fuelling your sense of purpose
- You reinforce your passion or re-connect with your lost passion
- You invigorate a sense of belongingness yourself, your family, the planet, and the creator.
- You wake up to new realities of life and respond most productively.
- You enliven the sense of joy, pleasure, and bliss in everything you opt to do.

Re-inventing requires you to review your goals, your mission. You got to be ready to renew the lens you have been using to see the world and refurbish your ideas. The scenario around you is changing fast. So should you. Are you prepared to recapture the positivity, creativity, and curiosity?

RE-INVENTING CHALLENGE

I always try to give my own album space in between, so I have time to create a new sound and give people time to miss me. You have to come out fresh and re-invent yourself.
Akon

Re-inventing yourself is the most critical step in living your best life. For some people, the very idea of re-inventing stimulates a series of refreshing thoughts in mind. They are excited to see the flash of new possibilities. Re-inventing triggers an endowing sense of new choices of feeling, behaving, and thinking.

On the other hand, few people feel intimidates. They feel threatened by the changes they will have to go through. They feel terrified. They show resistance. They don't want anything to push them for change. They foresee pain, stress, and pressure. Instead of embracing the idea of 're-inventing', they become defensive and self-protective.

Failing to respond to the call of re-invent will keep you where you are. The brutal fact is, if you remain where you are, you will not reach where you want to be.

Purposeful life demands you to create a new you regularly. Passion-filled pursuits require constant re-formulation of your ideas, thoughts, and action. A performance-driven environment urges you to device new strategies to up your game, originate novel ways of outpacing everyone in the race.

Re-inventing is a daunting goal. It requires courage, confidence, and belief. Be ready for the knife of change. Bring a new sense of spark in your life. Find out new passions to pursue your purpose.

THREE LEVELS OF RE-INVENTING

When things are bad, it's the best time to re-invent yourself.
George Lopez

Re-inventing yourself will take place at three levels: thinking, feeling, and actions. Any effort to re-invent will be fruitless until it sparks revivification of the way you think, feel, and act.

Level #1
HOW YOU THINK?

Re-inventing starts from the way you think. Re-thinking the way you think would be a great start. To re-invent, you will have to reconstruct your thinking about yourself, about others, your profession, and about the world.

On your path to re-invent yourself, you will discover new patterns of thinking. New methods of reflecting. Better ways of understanding. Seek some help form thinking gurus like Tony Buzan. His MindMapping techniques are mind-blowing.

Revitalizing your thinking would mean instilling a new set of attitudes and restoring our self-belief in the face of daunting challenges. Re-inventing thinking will prepare you to experience a refreshing aspect of who we are and sparking new energy to the following purpose.

Level #2
HOW YOU FEEL?

The feelings you have been experiencing most of the time have made you the kind of person you are. Quality of your life is the quality of your feeling. Do you feel empowering feelings most of the time? Are you trapped by negative, disempowering, and draining feelings?

To give your life a new design, you will have to provide yourself new powerful feelings. Instead of allowing your feelings to take you anywhere and then keeping you there for long intervals, take charge. Choose the feelings you want to experience. Choose to feel confident, vibrant, upbeat, and happy. Decide to rejuvenate your accomplishments. Celebrate your identity, dreams, and achievements, even failures.

Level #3
HOW YOU ACT?

When you restyle your thinking and feelings, your actions inevitably change. The way you think and feel about something will hugely influence the way you behave.

Re-inventing yourself means, acting differently. Acting in a way that takes you closer to your purpose and builds the right future for you. Taking a different action would challenge you to refresh your talents, abilities, and skills, regain focus to pursue the right ambitions, and explore new behavioral patterns.

FIVE AREAS OF RE-INVENTING YOURSELF

Refreshing the way you think, feel, and act is a brilliant move. Once your thoughts, emotions, and behaviors are revived; it is essential to translate this abundant energy in the following critical areas of your life.

1. YOUR PHYSICAL HEALTH:

You may revitalize your physical being by starting new routines or joining a health club. Are you deciding to opt for healthy eating and saying no to junk food?

Would you like to go for a full medical check-up, preventing you from any future diseases?

Do you plan to take frequent breaks, adequate rest, and try relaxation techniques?

2. YOUR FINANCIAL STATUS

Where do you find yourself on the financial path? Do you dare to bust some financial myths? Do you plan to do something about your savings bucket? What about your dreams bucket? What about investing more wisely or having a financial coach? Most successful people go bankrupt because of financial illiteracy.

3. YOUR FAMILY & RELATIONS

At times we lose the most valuable asset for the one that we think we need the most. Deciding to re-invent at this stage will save you from being at a stage where you are super rich but alone. Would you like to kindle a new spark in your relationship with your wife? Do you intend to spend more time with your kids? Did you sensitize the importance of having selfless friends to you? What one regret you would like to avoid on your last day of life.

4. YOUR INTELLECTUAL CAPACITY

Do you wish to learn new skills? Want to finish what has been on your reading list for long? You desire to master critical knowledge? You wish to learn new thinking tools? You feel the need to expand your creative potential?

5. YOUR SPIRITUAL CONNECTION

Did you feel the need to connect with your creator? Have you been taking this connection for granted? Is the connection still working? How can you further strengthen this connection? What you need to ensure that the connection never weakens?

07 BASICS OF RE-INVENTING

When you dance, your purpose is not to get to a particular place on the floor. It's to enjoy each step along the way. Wayne Dyer

1. Self-awareness
2. Clarity of direction
3. Readiness to change
4. Openness to ideas
5. Hunger for feedback
6. Eagerness for learning
7. The flexibility of attitude and behavior

SEVEN TOOLS FOR RE-INVENTING

As an actor, you always have to re-invent yourself or end up in the gutter somewhere. It's my job to always change people's minds. I've known that for a long time, and I've had to do it.
Dylan McDermott

Tool #1
BRISK STINT

Most of us are caught in the trap of day-to-day unrewarding routine. Re-inventing will not occur automatically. It will require effort. Consistent effort. Daily.

I have a personal secret for my own revivification daily. I call it *Brisk Stint*.

What is *Brisk Stint*?

Brisk Stint is not a technique; it is a binder that dedicates a quick spell dedicated 100% for yourself. *Brisk Stint* is aimed at revitalizing yourself.

It is a spell when you choose to slow down and enjoy silence and peace of mind. *Brisk Stint* is basically *your appointment with yourself*. Once you start *meeting* yourself daily, you begin to experience serenity. You are unruffled, at ease, in control, and relaxed.

You need to realize that you are not indispensable. Graveyards are full of people who thought they were indispensable. Take time out for yourself, spend some quality moments with *you*. Revitalize and re-energize yourself. Replenish yourself with empowering thoughts.

When I started using this principle, it changed my life forever.

I build this painful realization that my audience, readers, coaches, business, career, colleagues, clients, and family will not get the best out of me until I can bring a renewed sense of spark, excitement, and flicker. This glint requires only 60 minutes a day from you.

Use this *'power hour'* every day to reinvigorate your physical, social, emotional, mental, and spiritual being. Choose to read books, chase a new hobby, master a foreign language, grow your computer skills, jump a business, devote time to fitness activities. And taste a new sense of being.

Tool #2
AFFIRMATIONS

We all talk to ourselves almost all the time. However, positive self-talk can revitalize your thinking and actions.

You can use the following affirmative phrases to boost your energy levels:

- I am calm and relaxed.
- I deserve to feel good right now.
- I feel grounded and fully present.
- I can effectively handle any situation that comes my way.
- I am grateful for all the positive things in my life.
- My body is healthy and robust.
- I enjoy eating delicious and healthy food.
- I exercise regularly in a relaxed and enjoyable manner.
- I think thoughts that uplift and nurture me.
- I enjoy thinking about positive thoughts.

Tool #3
SELF-ESTEEM TALK

I have written the below affirmations to help you boost your self-esteem and confidence:

- I am a beautiful and worthy person.
- The world around me is full of radiant beauty and abundance.
- I am filled with energy, vitality, and self-confidence.
- I care for my emotional and physical well-being.

- I love and honor my body, and I listen to my body's needs
- I fill my mind with positive and self-nourishing thoughts.
- I deserve health, vitality, and peace of mind.
- I have total confidence in my ability to heal myself.
- I feel infused with abundant energy and vitality.
- I am attracted only to those people and situations that support and nurture me.
- I appreciate the positive people and situations that are currently in my life.
- I love and honor myself.

Tool #4
PHYSICAL RELAXATION

Regular exercise can be a great stress-buster. You should also go for a brisk walk, play tennis, swim, or engage in some other active sport.

It will not only relax and re-energize your body but also boost your immune system.

Do something you enjoy for at least 30 minutes a day, five days a week.

- Try boxing, kickboxing, or a punching bag exercise; it helps you release your built-up tension.
- Benefit from yoga, deep breathing exercises, stretching, martial arts, and meditation, as they all have built-in relaxation techniques.
- Involve yourself in doing something you love doing, such as hiking, skiing, dancing, roller-skating.

Don't overdo physical activity. Trying to do too much could be mentally and physically stressful.

Tool #5
DEEP BREATHING

The more oxygen you draw in, the less tense, short of breath, and anxiety you will feel. So the next time you need to re-charge yourself, take a minute to slow down and breathe deeply. You will instantly perceive the following benefits:

- Quickly boosts energy levels
- It's simple, yet powerful
- Can be practiced almost anywhere

Sit comfortably with your back straight. Place one hand on your chest and the other on your stomach. Breathe in through your nose, and the hand on your stomach should rise. The hand on your chest should move very little.

Exhale through your mouth, pushing out as much air as you can while contracting your abdominal muscles. The hand on your stomach should move inwards as you exhale, but your other hand should move very little. Continue to breathe in through your nose and out through your mouth. Try to inhale enough air so that your lower abdomen rises and falls. Count slowly as you exhale.

If you find it hard to breathe from your abdomen while sitting up, try lying on the floor. Place a small book on your stomach, and try to breathe so that the book rises as you inhale and falls back as you exhale.

Slowly take a deep breath for a count of 7, breathe out for a count of 11. Continue 7-11 breathing until your heart rate slows down, your sweaty palms dry off, and you begin to experience a feeling of relaxation all through your body.

Tool #6
MEDITATION

Regular practice of meditation actually empowers your brain, dispels negativity and stress and build up the feelings of joy and relaxation.

Before commencing meditation, ensure four things: a quiet place, the right posture, an object to focus on, and a watchful attitude.

Pick a calm place in your home, office, garden, place of worship, or outdoors, where you can relax without distractions or interruptions. Sit up with your spine straight, either in a chair or on the floor. You can also try a cross-legged or lotus position. Avoid lying down as this may lead to you falling asleep, but ensure that you are sitting in a comfortable position.

Choose to focus on an object in your surroundings to enhance your concentration. You can close your eyes and pick up a meaningful word or phrase and repeat it in your mind. If distracted, gently turn your attention back to your point of focus. Do not be bothered about disturbing thoughts. Do not fight them, just keep focused.

SIMPLE MEDITATION

Sit or lie in a comfortable position. Close your eyes and breathe deeply. Let your breathing be slow and relaxed. Focus all your attention on your breathing. Notice the movement of your chest and abdomen in and out.

As you inhale, say the word 'peace' to yourself, and as you exhale, say the word 'calm.' The word 'peace' should sound like p-e-e-a-a-a-c-c-c-e-e-e. The word 'calm' will sound like c-a-a-a-l-l-l-l-m-m-m.

Repeating these words as you breathe in will help you to concentrate. Continue this exercise until you feel very peaceful.

OAK TREE MEDITATION

Close your eyes and breathe deeply. Seated in a comfortable position, let your breathing be slow and relaxed. Imagine that your body is like a healthy oak tree. Your body is firm like the solid brown trunk of the tree. Imagine powerful roots growing from your legs and going down deep into the earth, anchoring your body sturdily.

You feel stable and robust, *able to handle any stress.* Every time you are invaded by upsetting thoughts or situations, visualize your body remaining grounded like the oak tree. Feel the vigor and solidity in your arms and legs. Now you feel confident and relaxed, able to handle any state of affairs.

STRING MEDITATION

After deep breathing, imagine a thick, full string attaching itself to the base of your spine. Make sure your string is full and strong enough. Then imagine a thick metal hook attaching itself to the end of your string.

Now visualize your grounding string dropping down two hundred feet below the earth's surface and hooking on to the solid bedrock below the earth. Continue to breathe deeply and feel the peace and stability your grounding string can bring you.

Tool #7
RELAXING MUSCLES

Lie on your back in a comfortable position. Allow your arms to rest at your sides, palms down, on the surface next to you. Inhale and exhale slowly and deeply. Clench your hands into fists and hold them tightly for 15 seconds. As you do this, relax the rest of your body.

Then let your hands relax. On relaxing, you will feel a golden glow flowing into your entire body, making all your muscles soft and flexible. Now, alternately tense and relax the following parts of your body: face, shoulders, back, stomach, pelvis, legs, feet, and toes. Hold each part tensed for 15 seconds and relax your body for 30 seconds before going on to the next part.

Finish the exercise by shaking your hands and imagining the remaining tension flowing out of your fingertips.

SUMMARY

Remember, re-inventing in not a once in a lifetime activity. To secure victory, you have to consistently outgrow your limits, hurdles, and blockades. You don't have to remain today who you were when you began this chase. Make a firm commitment to take the full advantage of the tools provided you in the latter part of this chapter. If you are serious about living your purpose and passion for optimizing performance, you will be required to constantly 're-invent' yourself – almost daily.

FINISH STRONG

Most of us are perfect initiating changes but really bad at following it through to the finish line.

You have learned a concrete philosophy and hands-on principles to win through to an extraordinary life.

The focal point is to stop playing the blame game and start turning your life around today. You are being sensitized to abandon all your excuses and start making things happen.

You have been provided several tools and strategies as well to make your vision a reality. However, nothing will change until your daily actions reflect the essence of Tick Tick Dollar philosophy. If you feel an inner resistance to take the leap, remember: *failing to act is acting to fail.*

After working with thousands of people over the last fourteen years, in my experience, people in your situation will take either of the two steps:

1. Not taking action at all
2. Taking the wrong actions

Not acting is dangerous, but acting in the wrong direction can be an absolute killer. I recently ran into one of my cousins, Munir, who is battling severe problems in almost all the four vital areas of his life: work, finance, family, and health. I asked him the same questions that my coach Jim Rohn had asked me a few years ago, which had changed my life.

'How long have you been working?' I asked.

'Since my childhood. I never attended any school.' He answered.

'How many years precisely?'

'About twenty-five years,' was his answer.

'Twenty-five years! Wow!' I was amazed. 'And how much money have you saved in the last twenty-five years?' I quizzed him.

'Nothing,' was his pat reply.

'And how much money have you invested in the last twenty-five years?'

'Not a single penny,' he admitted sheepishly.

His response caught me by surprise. My shock increased, and I could not resist asking, 'Who sold you this plan?'

'What do you mean?' my cousin asked, puzzled.

'I mean, how can you continue to work with a policy or a plan that has brought you to a stage where you are still struggling after working twenty-five years?' I queried.

People keep moving in a direction that takes them precisely nowhere. How can anybody be practically penniless, with deteriorating health and damaged family relations after two-and-a-half decades of hard work? Had he been living some of the principles presented in this book, this would not have been the case.

SURVIVAL VS. FREEDOM

As you move to the finish line, you can direct your energies at one of these choices:

1. Striving for survival
2. Striving for freedom

People who have no commitment to success are busy finding a way to survive. They just want to 'get through the day.' This narrow focus does not allow them to think beyond today. They remain trapped in the issues and problems of day-to-day living. Without a doubt, these people successfully touch the poverty line. Sometimes they sink even one step lower, slipping below the poverty line. Since their goal is merely to exist, they somehow manage to achieve this goal.

They cannot visualize the consequences of their unwise decisions and actions on their families' future and careers. They waste energy on things that are neither directly relevant to them nor useful for anyone else. If your daily focus is merely on survival, you can never come up with the plans and strategies that can prepare you for a breath-taking future.

On the other hand, if you are serious about living a purpose-based, passionate life, filled with success, prosperity, and achievement, you will live with focus and momentum. You will always think long term. Your focus will never be on sheer survival. You will devote your time and energy to boom, flourish, and thrive. You will invest resources in exploring opportunities that can lead you to a great life. Despite the day-to-day problems, issues, and setbacks, you will not give up. You will stand tall, confront the crisis, and never choose a solution that only gives you short-term results while damaging your career, success, and reputation in the longer run.

Instead of indulging in idle gossip about people and things, you would prefer to discuss ideas that can be life-changing. When your wide-ranging focus is on creating freedom for yourself and your family, you somehow manage to *earn* the freedom that brings prosperity, success, and accomplishment.

RISE FORMULA

> *"Even if I don't finish, we need others to continue.*
> *It's got to keep going without me."*
> *Terry Fox*

Inspiration without action is of no use. Let me equip you in the end with a potent execution tool, RISE model. Once you pick up an area for improvement in your life, RISE will allow you to see where you are, where you want to go, what necessary support you need, and how to keep yourself on track.

REALITY

The starting point is to face the brutal reality. For instance, you want to improve your physical health and fitness. The first step in initiating and sustaining this change is to neutrally see where you are in terms of your health. How do you rate it at a scale of 1-10? If it is terrible, how bad is it? You have to see the reality with a neutral eye. See the way it is. However, don't see it worse than it actually is.

INTENT:

Seeing reality may frustrate you. However, you immediately shift your focus on where do you want to be? What is your image of an ideal body? How would you like to be in terms of your stamina, energy, fitness, flexibility, residence, etc. Give your intent some image, picture, or a portrait.

> *"What I think a lot of great marathon runners do is envision crossing that finish line. Visualization is critical. But for me, I set a lot of little goals along the way to get my mind off that overwhelming goal of 26.2 miles. I know I've got to get to 5, and 12, and 16, and then I celebrate those little victories along the way."*
> *Bill Rancic*

SUPPORT

Of course, there is always a gap between where you are and where you would like to be. That involves some action. You will be required to systematize your efforts, regulate your energy, and adjust your aim to bring about the required changes.

The surest way to achieve and multiply results in the desired areas is to find people who can support you. A support group provides you the necessary motivation and moral reinforcement to continue. Make a deliberate effort to incorporate into your support group people who can be useful and play a constructive role.

Develop a mastermind group. You can also build a buddy system. Surround yourself with people who will encourage and challenge you. Be accountable to someone other than yourself. Apart from my company's advisory board, I have my personal advisory board consisting of friends and professionals. I regularly call and meet them to seek their guidance on significant challenges I face in my life. Another way is to get professional support in the form of coaching, mentoring, and training.

EXECUTE:

A vast majority of people fail in life because of missing the most critical link. This is a link between aspirations and results. Quality of your life is the quality of your execution. You are judged by what you accomplish, not by what you think.

Keep an eye on the results you are creating. Nothing can be changed unless you put plans into action, create methods to measure your progress. You can use charts, software, or anything else that will allow you to objectively track your progress. We all need feedback—it's the breakfast of champions.

Take responsibility for putting your plan into action by watching vigilantly, supervising carefully, and scrutinizing mercilessly!

FROM KNOWLEDGE TO ACTION

> *"Defeat doesn't finish a man, quit does. A man is not finished when he's defeated. He's finished when he quits."*
> Richard M. Nixon

We all own a massive *'knowledge zone'* equivalent to acres of land. Viewing the enormous size of this zone that we *possess,* we are clearly considered ultra-rich. We are admired and appreciated when it comes to disclosing our 'knowledge assets.' People around us are impressed with the magnitude of our properties.

However, most of us are found to be living in a petite, shabby, and tiny darkroom when we unveil our *'action zone'.* People around us are instantly unimpressed, uninspired, and unmoved. They are not mesmerized with the size of our 'knowledge zone' anymore. You know why because your credibility is not based on your knowledge but actions.

Most of us, sleepwalking through life, are so immersed in the knowledge zone that they don't have time to look into their action zones. Then comes a day when some unescapable incident triggers the need and forces you to visit your action zone. You feel shocked, ashamed, and even traumatized.

The painful encounter with reality in the action zone makes your restless. It gets so difficult for you to digest that the king of the knowledge city was a plain beggar in the 'action city.' Wouldn't it be hurting to know that a millionaire in knowledge currency turns out to be bankrupt in action exchange?

It reminds me of my physics class, where many students scored 100% in theory but didn't perform well in the 'practical.' And you know better than me that the overall result of those students was hard to take. They failed in the subject like we fail in the subject of *life*.

This is precisely how most of us are in real life too. We know a lot but act very less. We are generous in knowledge but miser in acting on that knowledge. When it comes to knowledge, we seem to own a whole city. But when it comes to putting into practice what we know, we are almost homeless. For the size of our knowledge city, we are seen as extremely wealthy, affluent, and prosperous. However, our action zone exposes that we are living below the poverty line.

Your success in life rarely depends on how much you know. It largely depends on how much you do. The size of your action zone should be more significant than the size of your knowledge zone. Your knowledge is rarely visible to others, but your actions always '*speak louder*' and, therefore, noticed by others.

If you continue to expand your action zone, you will automatically create a new zone for yourself. I call it 'experience zone,' a combination of your knowledge and action. This new zone belongs to you because this is '*your tested*' knowledge.

For most people on this planet, knowing and doing have always been two banks of the same river. Therefore, a vast majority fails to find a way of building a bridge between two essential pillars of their life.

Knowing something doesn't mean you will necessarily act upon it. There is a lot that we all know. But there is quite less that we act on. I can bet most of the stuff you read in this book may not be outside your 'knowledge zone.' But is it already inside your 'action zone'?

Success comes to those who gain knowledge, test this knowledge in their very own 'action lab,' and then, based on the results, create their own 'experience' zone. The secret of success is to have a constant supply of new knowledge. The stream should never stop; otherwise, you will be forced to act on the old knowledge, which can give you only old results.

Since the environment around you relentlessly changing, you need to take consistent action to try renewed knowledge in the lab. This requires the daily intensity to put whatever you know into practice.

You need to regularly update the 'experience zone' on the results and findings of your experiments in the action lab. Be generous in sharing your garden-fresh awareness, insights, wisdom, and experiences with the people around you to inspire and ignite them. When passing your experience to them, inspire them to test these renewed perceptions in their own 'action lab' and then continue the sharing process.

Remember, you can use your knowledge currency to impress others, but only your actions exchange can inspire. Knowledge is valued much in the school, but only your actions are valued in the marketplace. Knowledge will make you a scholar; actions will create a champion out of you. With the knowledge, you can win minds, but with superior actions, you can win hearts.

Whichever zone you focus more on will expand. If your knowledge zone is refreshing and the action zone is depressing, you will never succeed. Wake up before it is too late. You don't have to live like a king of knowledge and a panhandler of action? Take action to bridge your knowledge and actions and guarantee an unprecedented success for yourself and your loved ones.

1. Are you letting your actions speak louder than your knowledge?
2. Would you like to be remembered by your knowledge or by your actions?
3. Do you feel refreshed in your knowledge city and suffocated in the action room?
4. Which zone are you expanding more daily?
5. Is your current routine persuading you to be a *superstar* of knowing and an *extra* in doing?

1. Gain lots of new knowledge every day.
2. Activate your action lab to test knowledge, ideas, and perceptions for validity.
3. Take significant actions daily to turn your action room into a bustling city.
4. Grow the size of your action zone to match the size of your knowledge zone.
5. Show generosity to share your insights, awareness, and findings with others.
6. Publish your findings in the 'experience zone' with an expiry date on them.

If you didn't take action on this knowledge right *now*, beware that your current routine is persuading you to be a king of knowing and a beggar of doing.

Happy doing!

ACKNOWLEDGMENTS

It would be highly unfair if only my name appears on the cover of this book. I will acknowledge the role of so many other people whose talents and influence have made a significant impact on my life and work. From the bottom of my heart, I would like to thank all those who supported and helped me over the past few years as I embarked upon my voyage of self-discovery as a writer, motivational speaker, and entrepreneur.

First, my late parents for their vision and their ability to look beyond the challenges of the present and for imparting to me the right set of values, purpose and *training* to make a difference to the lives of those around me. I only wish they could have lived to see their faith in me rewarded by this book, and so much more.

My eldest brother Intzar Hussain, for his tireless support all through my journey to this incredible life. It was simply impossible without his fatherly love, encouragement and guidance. My heartiest thanks to my brothers, sisters, aunts, uncles, other relatives, and neighbors for their *unconditional* love and care. I will always remember your kindness and words of encouragement as well as your guidance and counsel all through my life.

My wife Rashda Abbas for being my biggest supporter in all my creative endeavors. She has stood shoulder to shoulder with me every step of the way. Thank you, Rashda, for allowing me the time and space to work on this project during the countless days, nights, weekends, and holidays that were required to complete this book. Most of all, I will never forget the pride you took in my progress; it was your encouragement that gave me the strength to continue on this journey.

My mother-in-law for being like a second mother to me, always ready to express her love and care. Words are inadequate to express how deeply appreciative I am of her warmth, kindheartedness and compassion.

There are many friends who deserve specific mention: Arif Anis, Farhan Masood, Sibtain Raza, Arif Zulqarnain, Mustafa Nagri, Shafaat Hashmi, Ahsan Khan, Ejaz Kamboh, Barkat Ali Nonary, Umair Iqbal Qureshi, Moazzam Shahbaz, Omer Ghani, Imran Haider, Syed Fakhar Ahmed, Abdul Sattar Babar, Usman Abid, Zubair Maya, Azfar Baig, Dr. Ebrahim Khalifa Aldosari, Khalid Malik, Azfar Ahsan, Hira Lal Bhawani, Rizwan Shah, Yousuf Usmani, Zafar Iqbal, S M Naveed, Zahid Nawaz, Baqir Jawa and Alexendar Truta for challenging me to do my best and for always being there for me.

My senior colleagues; Arif Anis Malik, Syed Zulfiqar Ali, Azhar Bokhari, Waqar Khadim, Dr. Naeem Mushtaq, Dr. Aatiqa Lateef, Bakhtiar Khawaja, Amer Qureshi, Taimur Afzal Khan, Hussain Jaffar, Dr. Amjad Saqib, and Saleem Jawad Alkhabori, for their unceasing support.

My fellow trainers and superstars of training industry; Arif Anis, Umer Khan, Farhad Karmally, Sohail Zindani, Wali Zahid, Umair Jaliawala, Andleeb Abbas, Sidra Iqbal, Muneeba Mazari, Noman Nasrullah, Nadeem Chowan, Ramiz Allawala, and for their continued support, idea exchange and encouragement.

My teachers and mentors; Masood Ali Khan, Dr. Sadaqat Ali, Arif Anis, Dr. Naeem Mushtaq, Philip S Lal, Dr. Rukhsana Kausar, Dr. Saima Ghazal, Max Babri, Naseem Zafar Iqbal, Aslam Khaliq, Kamran Rizvi, Dr. Seemin Alam, Dr. Hamid Sheikh, Dr. Najma Najam, Dr. Ruhi Khalid, Prof. Shehnila Tariq, Dr. Asim Sehrai, Prof. Badr Ismail, Prof. Majeed Malik, Dr. Naumana Amjad, and Dr. Jawaz Jaffri for believing in me and making me whatever I am today.

My clients for providing me the opportunity to contribute and to hone my learning models and methodologies; without them there would be no book.

Team *Possibilities* for their unwavering support throughout this assignment. My team has actually made this book possible.

- Arooma Fakhar, your support in orchestrating the research project behind this book is deeply appreciated.
- Nasir Tairq and Nisar Ali Gohar, your support in giving this book a real shape through flawless printing is deeply appreciated.
- Tausif Niazi for reviewing the book overnight and removing critical errors. Your support in research has been tremendous.

Mateen Hamza, who created world class illustrations for my books, is an excellent visual thinker. He takes my words and conceptualize them into hand-made doodles. His transformation of the ideas in this book into simple visuals will help readers to understand and retain more in the long run. Hamza's work can be seen at www.humorcarbons.com

Thanks to my publishing consultants Rick Alba and Michael March for their continued support and advice on helping me spread my message globally.

A special thanks to my personal coach, mentor and teacher; Dr.

Marshall Goldsmith (world #1 leadership coach) for gracing this book with his power-packed foreword. Thank you, Dr. Marshall for making a massive contribution to shape my current success. Your coaching philosophy has been the single most important element in bringing me where I am today.

I would also like to acknowledge the unconditional support of world #1 Management Guru, Dave Ulrich in my recent years of global growth. I can never forget your unparalleled encouragement when I first shared stage with you in Dubai at 43rd IFTDO Conference. You are a true teacher and an extraordinarily generous giver. Thank you for being my advisor in this journey of learning and growing.

It's a high time to express gratitude to the world #1 Creativity Guru, Tony Buzan, the Inventor of Mind Maps. Thank you for years of guidance especially for those 9 hours of uninterrupted personal coaching. I can never forget the moment when I made a mind-map of my dream life under your direct personal guidance and you awarded me with A++ rating on that. I am so happy to share with the world that the mind map of my dreams we co-created is turning fast into a reality.

I feel it mandatory on me to acknowledge the deep debt of gratitude I owe to my role models and mentors, especially Jim Rohn, Tony Robbins, Jack Canfield, Les Brown, Brian Tracy, Robin Sharma, Zig Ziglar, Nick Vujicic, Ram Charan, Marcus Buckingham, Roger Dawson, Jim Collins, and Dr. Wayne Dyer for instilling in me the courage, motivation and persistence to pursue my dreams. Their books and audio tapes have played a major role in shaping the present-day possibilities in my life.

This book is the fruit of listening to and learning from many people in both industry and academia who responded positively to my previous books, articles and training programs. Many of the ideas in this book originated from discussions with a host of people, ranging from my clients and professional associates to my teachers, close friends, workshop participants, colleagues, HR professionals and CEOs. I thank you all for helping me put this book on global map.

REFERENCES

1   Dr.Wayne W.Dyer, Manifest Your Destiny(1999), Harper Paprtback

2   Dr.Wayne W.Dyer, Your Sacred Self(2001), Harper Collins

3   Robertj.Herbold, Seduced By Success(1995), Jointly Adopted By Committee Of The American Bar

4   Dr.Wayne W.Dyer, Real Magic(2001), Harper Collins

5   Allen E. Fishman, 7 Secrets Of Great Entrepreneurial

6   Masters(2006), MacGraw.Hill

7   Daniel Goleman, Vital Lies Simple Truths(1986), Simon & Schuster

8   Chris Farmer, Business coaching(2007), Indiana Publlishing House

9   Donald J.Trump With Tony Schwartz, Trump The Art of The Deal(2007), The Random House Publishing

10 M. R. Kopmeyer, Heres Help(1990), Simon & Schuster

11 Dr. Donald E. Wetmore- Productivity Institute-website: http://www.balancetime.com Professional Member-National Speakers Association

12 Eric Allenbaugh Ph.D. Wakeup Calls(1994), Library Of Congress Cataloging in Publication

13   Ruth Sherman, Get Them To See It Your Way Right Away(2004), McGraw. Hill

14   Jamie Blyth With Jenna Glatzer, Fear Is No Longer My Relity(2005), McGraw. Hill

15   Harvard, Coaching And Mentoring(2004), Harvard Business Press

16   Mark H. McCormack, What They Still Don't Teach You at Havard Business School(1989), Bantam Books New York

17   Anthony Robbins, Unlimited Power(1997), Simon & Schuster

18   Dr.Wayne W.Dyer, Your Erroneous Zones(1976), Funk & Wagnalls New York

19   Steve Andreas & Charles Faulkner, NLP The New Technology of Achievement(2004), William Morrow & Co.

20   Vera Peiffer, Stress Management(1996), Thorsons

21   Jose Silva, The Silva Mind Control for Business Managers(1986), Simon & Schuster

22   Gerald Holton (4 December 2004). "Robert K. Merton - Biographical Memoirs" (PDF). *Proceedings of the American Philosophical Society* 148 (4): 506–517. http://www.aps-pub.com/proceedings/1484/480411.pdf.

23   http://time-management.bestmanagementarticles.com

24   Lucas and Carri http://www.lucasandcarricantoni.com

25   Michelle Zelig Pourau Master Relationship Coach http://www.personalpowerinternational.com/default.html

26   Stuart Crawford 'What Is The True Measure Of Time?'

ABOUT POSSIBILITIES

Possibilities® is a globally recognized Consulting Group known for Leadership Coaching, Team Building and Sales Transformation. Our 400 plus clients include many Fortune 500 companies in over 30 countries. Some of our key clients include Nestle, GE, Toyota, PepsiCo, Total, Abbott, Unilever, US Embassy and World Bank.

For details, please visit: www.possibilitiesglobal.com

EXECUTIVE EDUCATION

For over a decade and a half, Possibilities' team of Coaches, Consultants, Advisors, and Trainers have been committed to helping organizations achieve peak performance, growth, and greatness. Our team is continually researching to find out the key elements that make businesses grow and then assisting clients in putting those elements at work.

New skills and insights infused in our client-specific programs have helped nearly 400 organizations and businesses in various parts of the world. In our highly structured interaction, we partner with our clients and encourage them to.......

- Challenge conventional thinking about business, management, change, motivation, leadership, and organizational effectiveness.
- Empower the best talent by multiplying their ability and potential to contribute to the future success of your organization.
- Enable the executive team to make tough business decisions, manage ambiguity, anticipate complex future challenges, and implement new initiatives to build a culture of results.

CUSTOMIZED LEARNING IS OUR FORTE:

To help your organization capitalize on business opportunities available in the market, Possibilities tailors each program to meet your exact organizational, team, and business requirements.

Our approach is simple; each organization is different, so are its people, its challenges, and its opportunities. Therefore, every program that our facilitators' craft is different aimed to solve your business issues, and help your people speed up and drive business growth.

WHY POSSIBILITIES' CUSTOMIZED LEARNING EXPERIENCES?

Our repeat-business rate is 100%. Below is some crucial reason why our clients re-engage us year after year for their team's learning needs:

1. We run an in-depth need analysis before a learning intervention. Our approach suggests a shift from training to the partnership. We engage our clients from day one and jointly develop the program design and delivery strategies.
2. We don't leave the client until we help the client assess the benefits through our post-learning reinforcement process.
3. We utilize a flexible approach toward program design, format, duration, schedules, content, and even the learning methodology.
4. We have a diverse team of facilitators, experienced in running programs with a broad mixture of companies, always ready to challenge, broaden, and expand the thinking of your key people.

For Proposals, please write at info@possibilitiesglobal.com

EXECUTIVE COACHING

At Possibilities, we strongly believe that coaching can be a game changer for the individual growth and organizational success. Over the past one and a half decade, we have helped executives and leaders produce transformational results for themselves and for the organizations and communities they operate in.

Our passionate team of Coaches has not only developed an in-depth understanding of the coaching process but also unparallel expertise to ensure results in every coaching relationship.

Being one of the largest and fastest growing Coach Network in the region, we take pride in being obsessive about helping our clients succeed. Our philosophy is simple – our coaches only succeed when our clients do.

COACHING STREAMS FOR EXECUTIVES

1. Executive Coaching
2. Leadership Coaching
3. Strategy Coaching
4. Talent Coaching
5. Transition Coaching

6. Critical Incident Coaching
7. Executive Presence Coaching

POSSIBILITIES COACHING PROGRAMS

Executive Coaching:

One-on-one Coaching Assignment with selected executives based on agreed objectives to address development needs. The progress is measured on a quarterly basis. With over 200 Coaches in our network, we guarantee that no matter what issues or challenges your executives might be facing; we will present to you a wide range of options to choose your best coach to work with your leaders.

Coaching Certification

This is for organizations who want to build their internal team of certified coaches. Once you nominate your participants, our Coaches Team will evaluate them through a rigorous process before they get selected.

Qaiser and his coaches team takes them through a carefully designed learning journey offering both cutting edge theory and extensive coaching practice.

Coaching Skills for Leaders

Designed to help leaders take the best of what coaching has to offer - the dialogue, tools, and mindset—and leverage it to transform themselves, their teams and the organization. Participants of this program will learn to spot and take advantage of daily opportunities to think like a coach, listen like a coach, talk like a coach and act like a coach.

Management By Coaching

Coaching approaches can be used to make normal managerial conversations more productive. Career planning, performance reviews, job scoping, and so on—when coaching thinking is incorporated, these become more collaborative ventures. Consequently, the results are more likely to stimulate repeated action and engagement by those who are required to perform them.

Coaching for Team Performance

'Coaching for Team Performance' shows teams how to build team spirit, increase goal focus, reduce conflict and improve their working relationships. The program enables teams to focus on its real work, to achieve its business objectives. Team Coaching is about empowering the team to manage its own dialogue, in order to enhance its capability and performance.

Building a Coaching Culture

A coaching culture is not about "doing coaching" or the communication exchange between the coach and the Coachee. It's about how everyone in the organization interacts with each other in their everyday conversations. It's having the conversations that may not usually happen—across functions, across levels—to make sure we understand and can act in ways that amplify collaboration, agreement, and alignment.

For Proposals, please write at info@possibilitiesglobal.com

POSSIBILITIES FOUNDATION

The Possibilities Foundation was created in 2010 with the objective of unfolding possibilities of learning, and growth for the deprived segments of the community. Possibilities Foundation aspires to reach out to the forgotten segments of society, such as orphans, the aged, patients, prisoners, the disabled and the abandoned, to re-ignite in them the spark to dream, succeed, contribute and live life at its fullest.

INITIATIVES:

1. Education Support Program
2. Possibilities School
3. My First Bike -

All the author's proceeds from his books will go to Possibilities Foundation to support the education of underprivileged children.

For details, please contact at info@possibilitiesglobal.com
www.pf.org
www.qaiserabbas.org

Buy Qaiser's life changing books as a gift for your employees, customers, business associates, partners, suppliers, shareholders and other stakeholders.

All authors proceeds will go to **Possibilities Foundation** to educate underprivileged children.

You may also donate our books to libraries, schools, colleges, universities and vocational education institutes.

Printed in the United States
By Bookmasters